Mastering Chinese Characters:

A Modern Approach

汉字图解学习手册

David Su Liqun / 编著

商务印书馆
SINCE 1897　The Commercial Press
2014年・北京

图书在版编目(CIP)数据

汉字图解学习手册/苏立群编著.—北京:商务印书馆,2014
ISBN 978 - 7 - 100 - 10394 - 7

Ⅰ.①汉… Ⅱ.①苏… Ⅲ.①汉字—图解 Ⅳ.①H12-64

中国版本图书馆 CIP 数据核字(2013)第 262384 号

汉字图解学习手册

苏立群 编著

商 务 印 书 馆 出 版
(北京王府井大街 36 号 邮政编码 100710)
商 务 印 书 馆 发 行
北 京 中 科 印 刷 有 限 公 司 印 刷
ISBN 978 － 7 － 100 － 10394 － 7

2014 年 6 月第 1 版　　　　　开本 787×1092　1/32
2014 年 6 月北京第 1 次印刷　　印张 11⅛
定价:39.00 元

CONTENTS

PREFACE

During my twenty years teaching at SOAS (School of Oriental and African Studies, University of London) I began to develop an interest in different ways of teaching Chinese as a written language, but a serious attempt to explore the subject did not come about until 2004. Frequent interruptions meant that the work was only completed seven years later, in 2011. The following year, the Commercial Press in China agreed to be my publisher. It was with their unwavering support and practical advice that this handbook, 'Mastering Chinese Characters: A Modern Approach', was finally able to reach its current and final form.

Written Chinese has been taught traditionally by taking each character apart and tracing the roots of its radicals to their sources. Though fascinating for Chinese students already familiar with their own history and culture, this approach has not been particularly effective for foreign students learning the language from scratch. In hindsight, this strategy was perhaps both too academic and too localised. It tended to assume a basic knowledge of China—its national and folkloric heritage, its geography, social values and codes of behaviour.

In an attempt to avoid similar pitfalls, it became something of an obsession of mine to figure out an alternative way to inspire and support foreign students in our classes, a way which does not require prior knowledge of all things Chinese. The resulting handbook is an attempt at a more intuitive approach, one which employs fresh visual tools. As the saying goes, the novice monk has to be led through the temple door. Once over the threshold however, it would be up to him to pursue his own knowledge as far as his interest dictates. In time, it is quite possible, even likely, that the dedicated student would return to more traditional paths of academic pursuit. In this way, the handbook does not seek to replace valuable research and established practices, only to initiate the novice and to serve as a light-hearted aide memoire.

During the time between the first and last drafts of the text, we were fortunate to be able to put it to practical use in the classroom. The fact that almost all of the students were beginners was a huge bonus, and their response to the efficacy of the book was extremely constructive. This period of experimentation began on 18th June in 2012 and spanned three terms, the first and second of which catered for absolute beginners. Each term lasted 30 weeks, lessons were one and a half hours long, averaging 45 hours per term. The full three terms therefore required the commitment of 90 weeks to complete. After more than a year of study, the results of the final tests were encouraging. The students' average score was 72.9%, which meant that 608 out of 835 characters were successfully memorised, the equivalent of one every 4 minutes 45 seconds.

A result like this was possible because of a two-pronged approach: on the one hand, students were provided with basic knowledge of the development of Chinese writing from its inception in the Shang Dynasty until today; on the other, they were given tools with a contemporary flavour to enhance their memory.

At this point perhaps it is worth pointing out that the structure of Chinese characters mainly relies on three kinds of building blocks-pictograms 象形(4%) ideogrammic compounds 会意(13%) and phonosemantic compounds 形声(82%). The other three ways of building a character are less used. They are ideograms 指事, transformed cognates 转注, and rebus 假借 (all less than 1%).

Since both pictures and sound are regular components of Chinese characters, we have included a cartoon on every page, supported by a short piece of text in English where the students are encouraged to read aloud. Whatever proved most helpful to the class ended up on these pages, the priority being always practical use over established convention.

Right now, in the west, there seems to be tremendous interest in learning Chinese. In order to sustain this trend, it would seem prudent to focus on a couple of things: first, to remind those of us who are teachers that a spoken language and its written form are intimately connected. In other words, to teach the spoken language, it is paramount to teach reading and writing at the same time. Secondly, our attention ought to turn towards children and teenagers, for whom Chinese has become one of the most popular subjects at school. It is with this age group in mind that we hope to take on a serious subject in a relaxed and playful manner.

4

As this volume prepares to face the world, I would like to take the opportunity to thank all those who have given their time from conception to completion. I am grateful to the teachers at the school of Meridian Chinese Studies: Jian-Ling Shen(沈建玲) and Michelle Marshall(徐江秀);all the teachers who assisted in the lessons, including Jian-Ling Shen(沈建玲), Susie Zheng Liu(刘铮), and Si Chen(陈思), and the technical assistants Su Zi-han(苏子涵) and Maha H Ibrahim. I would also like to thank my poet friend Stephen Pucci and the artist Daniel Pheloung. Although their work does not appear in the final pages of the handbook, their generous contribution during the course of our journey was very much appreciated.

Finally, my special thanks extend to Carolyn Choa(蔡敏仪) whose thoughtful work on the English text in the 'read aloud' sections is invaluable.

This handbook is one of 6 volumes of work entitled 'Su's Origin of Language and Literature'(SOLL). The first volume being 'SOLL's TDR Zoom in Chinese Grammatical System'; the second, 'SOLL's Teaching of Chinese as a Foreign Language'; the third, which consists of four separate volumes, contains 'SOLL's TDR text books: Zoom In Mandarin Everyday Chinese for Beginners 1 to 3, and Lower Intermediate'; the fourth, 'SOLL's Selected Advanced Classical Studies'; the fifth, 'SOLL's Guide for Chinese as a Written Language—its Origins and Evolution'; and the last volume, 'A Compilation of SOLL Talks, Publications and Lectures'. The six volumes together total over a million words.

David Su Liqun

前　言

　　任教英国伦敦大学亚非学院（School of Oriental and African Studies, University of London）的20年期间，我一直都在寻找一种向欧美学生介绍汉字的方法。说起写"汉字图解学习手册"（以下简称"手册"）已经是2004年的事了，又由于中间时有其他的事情插进来，全书到2011年才完成，历时7年。2012年，商务印书馆表示愿意出版其中的一部分。其后，我得到了他们的大力支持和具体的指导，于是"手册"才会有今天的样子。

　　诚然，此书之前，也曾有人尝试过以"图片解析汉字"的方法来编写教材，不过总体来说收效不明显，原因是这些书对汉字的解释过于"学术化"与"地域化"。"学术化"是指"以文解文，以字解字"，忽略了读者对中国是"零知识"；"地域化"是指著书者大多对欧美受众群体的社会及价值观缺乏切身的了解，因而在文化的沟通和语言的表达两个方面都受到了局限。这本"手册"尽量避免这些短处，而采用了"授人以渔"的方法。第一，把学生领回到甲骨、金文和籀文时代，用汉字后面的故事来启发、引导学生；并且在选择和绘制卡通画的形象时，尽可能地与汉字的外观相贴近。第二，以"声"来加深学生对"字形"的记忆，在每一页中都设计了"把汉字说出来"的板块——用一句英文把这个汉字的形、声、义都归纳、融合进去，达到"只要记得住这句话，就知道这个字的意思、写法和发音"的目的。"手册"在图片的风格和诠释的语言方面尽量做到"本土化"，而且在"不伤及汉字筋骨"的原则下，用启蒙与幽默相结合的方式，达到"亦庄亦谐"的效果。另外我还在图片的下端加注了比较严谨的解释，这部分是用汉语写的，目的是让那些已经有了较高汉语水平的使用者更深地了解汉字。需要说明的是，这本手册的目的是普及汉字，而非学术研究。换句话说，在两者相冲突时，我取"普及"。

幸运的是"手册"从初稿的完成到最后交稿一年多的时间里，都一直能作为教本在课堂上使用。实验课程是从2012年6月18日起始，先后共三轮（第一、二轮是并行班），每轮30个星期计45个小时（每个星期上一个半小时的课）；三轮一共为90个星期。一年多的时间下来，测验的结果令人欣慰：在所教的835个汉字（含本书的300字）中，经过45个小时的学习，学生平均的成绩是能认识72.9%，即608个汉字。若以每分钟来计算，他们可以在4分45秒的时间内记住一个汉字。

在"手册"问世之际，我要衷心地感谢那些在"手册"成形的各个阶段都予以我诸多协助的子午文院的老师：沈建玲（Jianling Shen）和徐江秀（Michelle Marshall），在实验班中担任助教与统计的沈建玲、刘铮（Susie Zheng Liu）与陈思（Si Chen）老师以及在电脑技术上协助我的苏子涵和Maha H Ibrahim，还有我的诗人朋友Stephen Pucci 和美术家Daniel Pheloung等。

7

尤其要提及的是Carolyn Choa（蔡敏仪），她对手册英文部分"把汉字说出来"的整理与润色更是功不可没。

最后要说明，此次由商务印书馆出版的《汉字图解学习手册》是"苏氏文源丛书"中"汉字'解字说文'卷五"中的一部分。"苏氏文源"卷分为六：卷一，苏氏"天地人——趋真性汉语语法体系"；卷二，苏氏对外汉语教学理念与教学法；卷三，苏氏"天地人"对外汉语教本（初级本、中级本）；卷四，苏氏对外汉语古今文选（注释及评述）；卷五，汉字"解字说文"；卷六，苏氏文选（在世界各地的讲座、研讨论文以及报刊文章）。

苏立群

A QUICK GUIDE TO USING THE HANDBOOK

I. This handbook is suitable for :

1) Beginners living in English-speaking countries

2) Beginners who speak English but reside in other countries

3) Beginners living in China for whom English is their first language

4) Beginners living in China who speak English adequately

5) Chinese language teachers living in China or abroad

II. This handbook contains 300 characters

III. Reasons behind this selection:

1) They are the most frequently used Chinese characters

2) When the character exists in both full and simplified scripts, an explication is only given for the latter.

3) Most of the characters included are part of the official syllabus of the Chinese Proficiency Test(HSK) for beginners and intermediate students.

IV. How to use the handbook :

There are three different ways to look up a character :

1) Using English as a basis :

Say a student wants to look up the character for 'home', they would go to the letter 'H' to find the page number and then be directed to the character, 家.

2) Using Chinese radicals as a basis :

Employing the same example of 家—if the student can only remember the top part of the character, he will know that this radical contains 3 strokes. Sifting through all the radicals with this number of strokes will enable him to locate the one he requires, which will in turn lead him to the page for 家.

3) Using Pinyin as a basis :

If the student can remember the pronunciation of a character but not how it is written, he can look it up on the pinyin index. Using 家 as an example again, the pinyin for this character is 'jia', so the student will simply go to 'J' inside the pinyin index, then locate the relevant page.

V. Each page of the handbook contains 8 different pieces of information :

Using 家 as our example again :

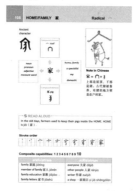

A. On the page header are :

1) The page number for the character No. 108

2) The English meaning of the character and the original form of the character. If there is a full script for the character, this would be given in brackets

3) The radical for looking up this character in a dictionary, in this case Radical宀

B. On the upper left hand corner are :

Ancient
character

It's the ancient character of 家.

C. In the middle of the page on the left are the character's structure, part of speech, and meaning. The top and bottom squares relate to its structure, to the left, its part of speech, and to the right, its meanings and nuances.

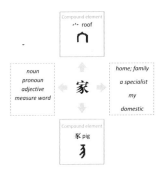

D. Moving to the right side of the page, from top to bottom are :

1) A cartoon reflecting the form and meaning of the character

2) The individual components which make up the character

$$家 = ⌒ + 豕$$

3) The structure of the character analyzed in Chinese, for those who already have a basic knowledge of the language

E. This is the READ ALOUD section where a simple line in English is offered as a light-hearted aide-memoire and to support the cartoon.

> 🌸 **READ ALOUD**
>
> In the old days, farmers used to keep their pigs inside the HOME. HOME is jiā (家).

F. At the bottom of the page is a demonstration of the stroke order for each character.

G. Degree of Composite Capability :

A number between 1-10 is assigned to each character depending on how often it is used as part of a term or phrase. In the case of 家, its capability is 10 because of its frequent and flexible usage.

Composite capabilities: 1 2 3 4 5 6 7 8 9 10

H. The character as prefix or suffix :

prefix/phrase	suffix/phrase
family 家庭 jiātíng	everyone 大家 dàjiā
member of family 家人 jiārén	other people 人家 rénjia
family education 家教 jiājiào	writer 作家 zuòjiā
family letters 家书 jiāshū	a shop 一家商店 yì jiā shāngdiàn

VI. The last section is for beginners who would like to explore the language further. Here, each character is grouped with some others related to it in sound, meaning or structure, presented in a simple diagram.

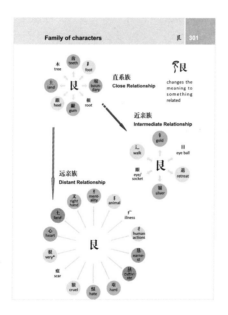

From the family album of 艮, we get to know some of its immediate family, cousins, and more distant relatives. These include 根, 跟, 眼, 银, 退, and很, all of which have an asterisk

13

next to them, meaning that these characters are also included in the handbook separately.

VII. All pronunciations follow the Official Pinyin. If a character has more than one pronunciation, the alternative is also given.

VIII. Frequently used terms and phrases :

1) When a character combines with others to form new terms and phrases,the most frequently used are included

2) If a character has multiple meanings, the most common usage is given

Index of Chinese Pinyin

Character	Pinyin	English	page
爱	ài	love	229
安	ān	peace; safety	103
八	bā	eight	52
把	bà	handle	128
办	bàn	manage; do	90
半	bàn	half	55
包	bāo	bun; wrap	77
饱	bǎo	be full	159
报	bào	report	129
被	bèi	quilt	245
本	běn	origin	193
比	bǐ	compare; compete	202
必	bì	certainly; must	183
边	biān	edge; side	113
表	biǎo	appearance	266
冰	bīng	ice	32
不	bù	not; no	8
步	bù	step; pace	204
菜	cài	vegetable	122
草	cǎo	grass	121
长	cháng/zhǎng	long; grow	21
唱	chàng	sing	142
超	chāo	surpass	284
吃	chī	eat	136
船	chuán	boat	280
春	chūn	spring	210
达	dá	reach	114
打	dǎ	strike	126

大	dà	big	123
单	dān	single	59
但	dàn	but	69
到	dào	arrive	47
道	dào	way; road	119
得	dé	obtain; get	151
灯	dēng	lamb	181
弟	dì	younger brother	58
点	diǎn	drop	176
电	diàn	electricity	249
定	dìng	stable	105
动	dòng	move	91
读	dú	read aloud	40
短	duǎn	short	256
对	duì	face	86
多	duō	many	155
饿	è	hungry	160
儿	ér	son; child	78
耳	ěr	ear	272
发	fā/fà	launch; hair	87
法	fǎ	law	97
饭	fàn	rice; food	158
房	fáng	house	187
飞	fēi	fly	26
非	fēi	wrong	18
分	fēn	divide	53
风	fēng	wind	238
服	fú	obey	232
敢	gǎn	dare	225
干	gàn/gān	trunk; dry	6
高	gāo	tall	30
告	gào	tell; inform	139
给	gěi	give	174
根	gēn	root	197
跟	gēn	heel	288
公	gōng	public	54
共	gòng	common	56
瓜	guā	melon	260

16

关	guān	shut; close	57
贵	guì	expensive	217
国	guó	country; state	148
果	guǒ	fruit	196
孩	hái	child	172
汉	hàn	the Han Nationality	93
好	hǎo/hào	good	165
号	hào	howl; bugle	132
喝	hē	drink	143
和	hé	harmony; peace; and	141
河	hé	river	98
很	hěn	very	150
后	hòu	behind	137
候	hòu	wait	75
化	huà	change	67
话	huà	word; speech	37
还	huán/hái	go back; still	115
回	huí	return	145
会	huì	meet	65
活	huó	live	99
火	huǒ	fire	180
己	jǐ	self	161
记	jì	remember	33
家	jiā	home; family	108
间	jiān/jiàn	between	112
见	jiàn	see	218
教	jiāo	teach; educate	226
角	jiǎo	horn	292
脚	jiǎo	foot	237
叫	jiào	yell; shout	133
觉	jiào/jué	sleep; sense	220
街	jiē	street	152
解	jiě	dissect	293
今	jīn	today; present	64
金	jīn	gold	295
近	jìn	shortcut; nearby	116
京	jīng	capital	29
九	jiǔ	nine	19

17

酒	jiǔ	wine	100
举	jǔ	raise; lift	4
开	kāi	open; start	9
看	kàn/kān	see; look after	246
考	kǎo	test	270
可	kě	can; be able to	134
客	kè	guest	107
空	kōng/kòng	empty	262
哭	kū	cry	200
老	lǎo	old	271
了	le/liǎo	a grammatical code	24
累	lèi	tired	252
离	lí	leave; keep away	31
李	lǐ	plum	194
里	lǐ	home; in; mile	285
理	lǐ	manager; put in order; reason	190
力	lì	power	89
历	lì	experience; go through	45
立	lì	stand; erect	242
练	liàn	practice	173
两	liǎng	two; 50 grams	14
路	lù	way; road	289
买	mǎi	buy	28
卖	mài	sell	43
忙	máng	busy	102
没	méi	disappear; not have	95
每	měi	every	241
美	měi	delicious; beauty	268
门	mén	door; gate	110
们	men	plural for mankind	68
米	mǐ	rice	269
面	miàn	face	16
民	mín	people	27
名	míng	name	138
明	míng	bright	208
木	mù	wood; tree	192
拿	ná	hold	223
奶	nǎi	milk; breast	164

18

男	nán	man	251
南	nán	south	44
难	nán/nàn	difficult	88
内	nèi	inside	48
能	néng	ability	236
你	nǐ	you	70
年	nián	year	23
鸟	niǎo	bird	261
您	nín	you	185
牛	niú	bull; ox	221
努	nǔ	put forth	92
女	nǚ	woman	163
胖	pàng	fat	235
跑	pǎo	run	287
朋	péng	friend	233
平	píng	flat; level	11
普	pǔ	universal; general	214
七	qī	seven	5
妻	qī	wife	167
奇	qí	strange	125
骑	qí	ride	175
起	qǐ	rise	283
气	qì	air	224
汽	qì	steam	96
千	qiān	thousand	20
前	qián	front	60
钱	qián	currency; money	253
亲	qīn	dear; close	243
请	qǐng	please; invite	41
秋	qiū	autumn	257
求	qiú	beg; pray	240
球	qiú	ball	191
去	qù	leave; go; apart	82
然	rán	right; correct	178
热	rè	heat	177
人	rén	people	63
日	rì	sun	205
容	róng	accommodate; hold	264

如	rú	similar; be like; as	166
伞	sǎn	umbrella	66
扫	sǎo	broom; sweep	127
山	shān	mountain; hill	149
上	shàng	up; above	7
少	shǎo/shào	few; young	131
身	shēn	body	291
生	shēng	born; produce	22
时	shí	time	207
识	shí	knowledge	35
实	shí	solid; practical	106
食	shí	food; eat	300
史	shǐ	history	135
使	shǐ	diplomat; use	74
世	shì	century; generation	12
事	shì	business; matter	15
视	shì	see; look at	188
是	shì	to be; yes	211
手	shǒu	hand	222
首	shǒu	head	61
舒	shū	comfort; stretch	277
数	shǔ/shù	count; math	227
双	shuāng	pair; dual	84
水	shuǐ	water	239
说	shuō	speak; talk	38
思	sī	think	184
四	sì	four	144
诉	sù	tell; accuse	36
算	suàn	count	278
太	tài	too; greatest	124
踢	tī	kick	290
题	tí	subject; topic	275
体	tǐ	body	71
天	tiān	sky; day	10
田	tián	farmland	250
甜	tián	sweet	276
条	tiáo	twig	195
听	tīng	listen	140

20

同	tóng	same; together	50
头	tóu	head	2
突	tū	suddenly; dash forward	263
土	tǔ	soil	120
团	tuán	group	146
退	tuì	retreat	118
外	wài	outside	154
完	wán	complete; intact	104
晚	wǎn	evening; late	213
王	wáng	king	189
网	wǎng	net	51
位	wèi	place; position	72
文	wén	character	179
问	wèn	ask	111
我	wǒ	I; me; self	201
舞	wǔ	dance	156
习	xí	practise	25
系	xì	tie; system	281
夏	xià	summer	157
先	xiān	ahead; first	80
鲜	xiān/xiǎn	fresh; rare	298
现	xiàn	appear; present	219
香	xiāng	fragrant; joss stick	258
想	xiǎng	miss; think	186
相	xiàng/xiāng	picture; see; each other	247
像	xiàng	image; be like	294
小	xiǎo	little; small	130
校	xiào	school	198
鞋	xié	shoe	299
谢	xiè	thank	42
心	xīn	heart	182
新	xīn	new	228
星	xīng	star	212
形	xíng	shape	153
姓	xìng	surname	168
须	xū	beard; hair	274
学	xué	study	171
眼	yǎn	eye; hole	248

羊	yáng	ram; sheep	267
页	yè	page	273
衣	yī	clothes	265
医	yī	medicine; doctor	46
椅	yǐ	chair	199
义	yì	justice	1
议	yì	discuss	34
易	yì	changing	209
因	yīn	reason	147
银	yín	silver	254
影	yǐng	shadow	216
应	yìng/yīng	respond	109
用	yòng	use	49
友	yǒu	friend	85
有	yǒu	have; exist	231
又	yòu	repeat; again	83
鱼	yú	fish	297
雨	yǔ	rain	296
语	yǔ	language; speak	39
育	yù	raise; nourish	234
元	yuán	element; unit	79
月	yuè	moon; month	230
云	yún	cloud	81
运	yùn	carry; motion	117
再	zài	again; once more	13
早	zǎo	morning	206
澡	zǎo	bath	101
站	zhàn	stand	244
张	zhāng	spread; stretch; open	162
真	zhēn	true; real	62
正	zhèng	right; make right	203
汁	zhī	juice	94
知	zhī	knowledge	255
中	zhōng	centre; middle	17
种	zhòng/zhǒng	plant; seed	259
主	zhǔ	main; host	3
住	zhù	reside; live	73
子	zǐ	child	169

自	zì	self	279
字	zì	character; words	170
走	zǒu	walk	282
足	zú	foot	286
最	zuì	most	215
做	zuò	do	76

Ancient character

Compound element

X arms
义

noun

adjective

义

justice; human relationship; meaning

righteous; adopted

Compound element

`、` justice (ideograph)

Note in Chinese

义 = **乂** + 丶

这是"義"的简体，一点代表真理，交叉部分暗示同心协力。

⚖ READ ALOUD

JUSTICE often requires a delicate balance and has to be handled with care. JUSTICE is yì（义）.

Stroke order

Composite capabilities: 1 2 3 4 5 6 7 8 9 10

prefix/phrase	suffix/phrase
an action for justice 义举 yìjǔ	justice 正义 zhèngyì
code of brotherhood 义气 yìqì	significance 意义 yìyì
	definition 定义 dìngyì

Ancient
character

Compound element
头 head

noun

measure word

adjective

proposition

头

head; top; end;
beginning; chief

first; leading

before

Compound element

Note in Chinese

头 = 头

这是"頭"的简
体。两点表示大脑
的思维，其余的部
分是头与身体。

🔊 READ ALOUD

It is not easy to stop ideas spinning around our HEADS all day. HEAD is
tóu（头）.

Stroke order

Composite capabilities: 1 2 3 4 5 6 7 8 9 10

prefix/phrase	suffix/phrase
head 头部 tóubù	in front 前头 qiántou
portrait 头像 tóuxiàng	behind 后头 hòutou
the first year 头年 tóunián	inside 里头 lǐtou
hair 头发 tóufa	bone 骨头 gǔtou

Ancient
character

Compound element

adjective

noun

verb

Compound element

main; primary

*host; owner;
master; person;
God*

*manage;
indicate;
advocate*

Note in Chinese

主 = 𤯞

原来是火柱，后来
成为占有的标志。

🌀 READ ALOUD

This character shows the flame slit on top of old military stations.
Surrounding towns later became the country's MAIN destinations for
trade. MAIN is zhǔ（主）.

Stroke order

Composite capabilities: 1 2 3 4 5 6 7 8 9 10

prefix/phrase	suffix/phrase
main 主要 zhǔyào	make decision 做主 zuòzhǔ
master 主人 zhǔrén	democracy 民主 mínzhǔ
take initiative 主动 zhǔdòng	Catholicism 天主教 Tiānzhǔjiào
sponsor 主办 zhǔbàn	

Ancient character

Compound element
兴 raise something/be excited

verb

noun

adjective

举

lift; raise; elect; start; cite

act; deed; move

entire

Note in Chinese

举 = 臼（兴）+￦ hand

这是"舉"的简体。上下都是赞成的手。

Compound element
 hand

🌐 **READ ALOUD**

Six RAISED hands secured the winning vote for this candidate. RAISE is jǔ（举）.

Stroke order

Composite capabilities: 1 2 3 4 5 6 7 8 9 10

prefix/phrase	suffix/phrase
hold 举办 jǔbàn	election 选举 xuǎnjǔ
movement 举动 jǔdòng	choose 推举 tuījǔ
raise one's hand 举手 jǔshǒu	report(an offence) 检举 jiǎnjǔ
throughout the world 举世 jǔshì	

Ancient
character

Compound element

七 seven

numeral

七

seven

Note in Chinese

七 = 七

两线垂直交叉后，
竖线向右边拐。

Compound element

✿ READ ALOUD

There are dangerous crossroads ahead. The speed limit is only SEVEN
miles per hour. SEVEN is qī（七）.

Stroke order

Composite capabilities: 1 2 3 4 5 6 7 8 9 10

prefix/phrase	suffix/phrase
July 七月 Qīyuè	in great disorder 乱七八糟
aged in late seventies 七老八十	luànqībāzāo
qīlǎobāshí	
be perturbed 七上八下	
qīshàngbāxià	

Ancient
character

Compound element

Ƴ

tree branches

adjective

adverb

verb

noun

gān: *dry*

gàn: *do*

trunk

Note in Chinese

干 = Ƴ + 十

一个简体替代了两
个繁体"幹"和
"乾"。有树的主
干的形象，也有晾
干衣服的晾衣架的
形象。

Compound element

十

tree trunk

- **🎵 READ ALOUD** -

This character looks like the TRUNK of a tree with branches. TRUNK is
gàn（干）.

Stroke order

Composite capabilities: 1 2 3 4 5 6 7 8 9 10

prefix/phrase	suffix/phrase
police 干警 gànjǐng	work hard 苦干 kǔgàn
work 干活 gànhuó	able 能干 nénggàn
dry-clean 干洗 gānxǐ	get right on the job 实干 shígàn
dry fruit 干果 gānguǒ	dry off 吹干 chuīgān

Ancient
character

Compound element

⊥ above

noun

verb

preposition

上

upper; higher;
last; most;
recent; first

come up; get on;
go to; go ahead;
enter; supply; be
carried on; be
engaged...

on; within; in; at;
formerly; above;
up...

Compound element

Note in Chinese

上 = ⊥

这个字形很形象，
加的一横表示在上
边。

🔊 **READ ALOUD**

A tall building rises UP from the ground towards the sky. UP is
shàng（上）.

Stroke order

Composite capabilities: 1 2 3 4 5 6 7 8 9 10

prefix/phrase	suffix/phrase
above 上头 shàngtou	morning 早上 zǎoshang
climb mountain 上山 shàngshān	evening 晚上 wǎnshang
go to school 上学 shàngxué	on the street 街上 jiēshang
in the sky 上空 shàngkōng	above water 水上 shuǐshang
go on-line 上网 shàngwǎng	

Ancient character

Compound element
— sky

adverb

不

no
not

Note in Chinese

不 = 一 + 𠚍

下边是一只鸟，上
面一横表示天。

Compound element
𠚍 bird

READ ALOUD

When birds migrate, they will NOT be seen again until the following year.
NOT is bù（不）.

Stroke order

Composite capabilities: 1 2 3 4 5 6 7 8 9 10

prefix/phrase	suffix/phrase
is not exist 不在 búzài	absolutely not 绝不 juébù
don't eat 不吃 bùchī	
is not 不是 búshì	
is not beautiful 不美 bùměi	

Ancient character

Compound element

— door bolt

verb

noun

adjective

开

open; lift; start; leave; write out; boil; make

parts; potion

Note in Chinese

开 ＝ 一＋ 丫丫

这是"開"的简体。
下面是两只手，上面
一横是门闩。

Compound element

丫丫 two hands

🐟 READ ALOUD

Two hands are needed to shift the heavy bolt and OPEN the doors. OPEN is kāi（开）.

Stroke order

Composite capabilities: 1 2 3 4 5 6 7 8 9 10

prefix/phrase	suffix/phrase
open the door 开门 kāimén	open 打开 dǎkāi
start 开始 kāishǐ	walk away 走开 zǒukāi
open and clear 开朗 kāilǎng	open wildly 开开 kāikāi
joyous 开心 kāixīn	

Ancient character

Compound element
— sky line

noun

adjective

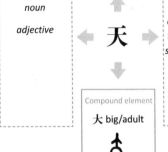

天

sky; heavens;
day; a period of
time in the day;
season; weather;
nature; God

natural; inborn

Compound element
大 big/adult

Note in Chinese

天 = 一 + 大

"大" (P123大)
字上面加一横，表
示大到了极限就是
"天"。

🔊 **READ ALOUD**

When we think big, the SKY is the limit! SKY is tiān（天）.

Stroke order

Composite capabilities: 1 2 3 4 5 6 7 8 9 10

prefix/phrase	suffix/phrase
sky 天空 tiānkōng	sunny day 晴天 qíngtiān
weather 天气 tiānqì	Sunday 星期天 xīngqītiān
innate 天生 tiānshēng	each day 每天 měitiān
natural 天然 tiānrán	hot day 热天 rètiān

Ancient
character

Compound element

平 flat/level

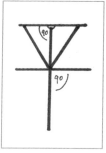

adjective

verb

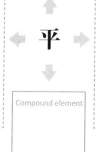

level; flat; even;
smooth

make level; be on
the same level;
make the same
score; equal;
calm; put down;
average

Compound element

Note in Chinese

平 = 乑

这个字演示着一个
平稳坚固的结构。

💿 READ ALOUD

This character with two FLAT lines is evenly balanced on both sides. FLAT
is píng（平）.

Stroke order

Composite capabilities: 1 2 3 4 5 6 7 8 9 10

prefix/phrase	suffix/phrase
safe and sound 平安 píng'ān	fair 公平 gōngpíng
calm down 平定 píngdìng	unusual 不平常 bùpíngcháng
the ordinary people 平民 píngmín	standard 水平 shuǐpíng
usually 平日 píngrì	
in normal times 平时 píngshí	

Ancient
character

Compound element

three times
of ten

noun

世

*lifetime; life;
generation; age;
the world*

Compound element

Note in Chinese

世 = 卋

按中国古代的算法，
一个十字代表一代，
大约三十多年；三
个十字表示三代，
连在一起便是一个
世纪，也表示人的
一生。

🔊 READ ALOUD

Three generations more or less makes a CENTURY. CENTURY is shì（世）.

Stroke order

    世

Composite capabilities: 1 2 3 4 5 6 7 8 9 10

prefix/phrase	suffix/phrase
century 世纪 shìjì	come into the world 出世 chūshì
world 世界 shìjiè	dead 去世 qùshì
in the world 世上 shìshàng	way of life 处世 chǔshì
	all one's life 一生一世 yìshēngyíshì

Ancient character

Compound element

 trap/net

adverb

再

again; then;
once more;
only then;
in addition;
on the top of
that; no matter;
how...still

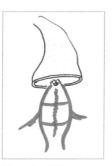

Note in Chinese

再 = 人 + 冃 + 二

除了第一画的横，
下面是一条鱼。横
表示一个网，鱼儿
一再入网，不记教
训。

Compound element

the head of
fish + second
time

🍥 READ ALOUD

If the fisherman throws his net into the sea AGAIN and AGAIN, he is sure
to catch more than he needs for supper. AGAIN is zài（再）.

Stroke order

Composite capabilities: 1 2 3 4 5 6 7 8 9 10

prefix/phrase	suffix/phrase
goodbye 再见 zàijiàn	repeatedly 一再 yīzài
over and over again 再三 zàisān	
besides 再说 zàishuō	

Ancient character

Compound element

— one object

numeral

noun

measure word

two; a few; some

both; either; neither

a traditional unit of weight 50 grams

Compound element

 equal

Note in Chinese

两 = — + 㒳

这个字显示把一个空间平均分配给两个人。

🔊 READ ALOUD

TWO equal spaces are created out of a single room. TWO is liǎng（两）.

Stroke order

Composite capabilities: 1 2 3 4 5 6 7 8 9 10

prefix/phrase	suffix/phrase
two halves 两半 liǎngbàn	weight 斤两 jīnliǎng
two piece of 两个 liǎng gè	
both sides 两边 liǎngbiān	
dual purpose 两用 liǎngyòng	

Ancient character

Compound element

屮 + 日
official + duty

noun

verb

事

matter; trouble; job; responsibility

be engaged in; serve

Compound element

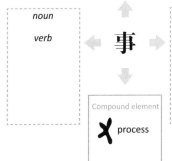

ㄨ process

Note in Chinese

事 = 屮+日+ㄨ

这个字是取上边的
"吏"（公务）的
一半，加上下边的
"手"，表示动
手处理人与物的
"事"。

READ ALOUD

The daily BUSINESS of a government official included processing a lot of documents by hand. BUSINESS is shì（事）.

Stroke order

Composite capabilities: 1 2 3 4 5 6 7 8 9 10

prefix/phrase	suffix/phrase
matter 事情 shìqing	have an accident 出事 chūshì
fact 事实 shìshí	story 故事 gùshi
accident 事故 shìgù	sensible 懂事 dǒngshì
it all depends on human effort	
事在人为 shìzàirénwéi	

Ancient
character

Compound element
首 face

noun
verb
measure word
adverb
adjective

面

face; surface; side; noodle
directly
soft

Compound element
冂 shape

Note in Chinese

面 = 首 + 冂

这个字的中间是人
的鼻子，两面是面
颊，上边的一横表
示头发。

READ ALOUD

This person's FACE resembles a pumpkin! FACE is miàn（面）.

Stroke order

Composite capabilities: 1 2 3 4 5 6 7 8 9 10

prefix/phrase	suffix/phrase
face to face 面对面 miàn duì miàn	meet 见面 jiànmiàn
meet face to face 面谈 miàntán	aspect 方面 fāngmiàn
bread 面包 miànbāo	outside 外面 wàimiàn
noodles 面条 miàntiáo	meet personally 见一面 jiàn yí miàn

Ancient character

verb

noun

Compound element

中 *in the middle*

中

Compound element

中

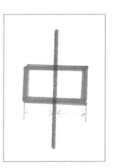

Note in Chinese

中 = 中

将一个长方形从中间分成两等份。

zhōng: middle; centre; in; among; intermediate; mean; halfway; in the process of...

fit for

zhòng: hit

🐝 READ ALOUD

A CENTRE line divides this rectangle into two equal parts. CENTRE is zhōng（中）.

Stroke order

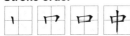

Composite capabilities: 1 2 3 4 5 6 7 8 9 10

prefix/phrase	suffix/phrase
China 中国 Zhōngguó	high school 高中 gāozhōng
in between 中间 zhōngjiān	in the book 书中 shūzhōng
lunch 中饭 zhōngfàn	at home 家中 jiāzhōng
Chinese language 中文 Zhōngwén	in the meeting 开会中
be hit by bullet 中弹 zhòngdàn	kāihuì zhōng

Ancient
character

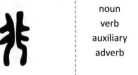

noun
verb
auxiliary
adverb

Compound element

a person

非

Compound element

ξ

a person

wrong;
not conform to;
non-; have
got to

Note in Chinese

非 = ⻖ + ξ

两个人背对背，表
示相互否定。

🔊 READ ALOUD

When two men disagree, each is likely to think that the other is WRONG.
WRONG is fēi（非）.

Stroke order

Composite capabilities: 1 2 3 4 5 6 7 8 9 10

prefix/phrase	suffix/phrase
illegal 非法 fēifǎ	right and wrong 是非 shìfēi
extraordinary 非常 fēicháng	no more than 无非 wúfēi
overstepping one's bounds 非分 fēifèn	

Ancient
character

Compound element

九 nine

numeral

noun

adjective

九

nine

many;
numerous

Compound element

Note in Chinese

九 =

这个十字交叉的一
横多弯，表示波折
很多，因此成为个
位数中最大的一
个。

🔊 READ ALOUD

Because of the three hairpin bends ahead, the speed limit is set at NINE
miles per hour. NINE is jiǔ（九）.

Stroke order

Composite capabilities: 1 2 3 4 5 6 7 8 9 10

prefix/phrase	suffix/phrase
September 九月 jiǔyuè strong gale 九级风 jiǔjífēng a drop in the ocean 九牛一毛 jiǔniúyìmáo	the third nine-day period after the winter solstice—the coldest days of winter 三九 sānjiǔ

Ancient character

Compound element

千 thousand

numeral

千

thousand;
a great amount
of

Compound element

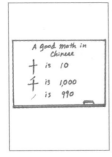

A Good math in Chinese
十 is 10
千 is 1,000
ノ is 990

Note in Chinese

千 = 千

十个百是千，十的
上面是一撇是指示
符，表示很多的
"十"。

READ ALOUD

Many tens make a THOUSAND. The stroke at the top denotes 'many'.
THOUSAND is qiān（千）.

Stroke order

Composite capabilities: 1 2 3 4 5 6 7 8 9 10

prefix/phrase	suffix/phrase
through the ages 千古 qiāngǔ	five thousands 五千 wǔqiān
a winged steed 千里马 qiānlǐmǎ	
every family 千家万户	
qiānjiāwànhù	
kilometre 千米 qiānmǐ	

Ancient
character

adjective

verb

noun

Compound element

 long/grow

长

chǎng: long;
length;
be good at...

zhǎng: older;
head; grow;
being to grow;
increase...

Compound element

Note in Chinese

长 = 乑

这 是 "长" 的 简
体，每 一 画 都 很
长，而 且 指 向 不 同
的 方 向。

❖ READ ALOUD

None of these LONG arrows are pointing the same way. LONG is
cháng（长）.

Stroke order

Composite capabilities: 1 2 3 4 5 6 7 8 9 10

prefix/phrase	suffix/phrase
length 长短 chángduǎn	the whole length 全长
Yangtze River 长江 Chángjiāng	quáncháng
the Great Wall 长城 Chángchéng	grow 生长 shēngzhǎng
long-term 长期 chángqī	grow up 成长 chéngzhǎng
grow up 长大 zhǎngdà	minister 部长 bùzhǎng

Ancient character

Compound element

↓ bud

verb

noun

adjective

adverb

↑
生
→

produce;
give birth;
be born; grow

life; pupil;
scholar

alive; green;
raw...

Compound element

一 earth

Note in Chinese

生 = ↓ + 一

下面是土（P120
土），上面是刚刚
破土出生的小芽。

READ ALOUD

A little bud grows out of the soil the same way a baby is BORN out of his mother's womb. BORN is shēng（生）.

Stroke order

Composite capabilities: 1 2 3 4 5 6 7 8 9 10

prefix/phrase	suffix/phrase
give birth 生育 shēngyù	be born 出生 chūshēng
produce 生产 shēngchǎn	Mr. 先生 xiānsheng
life 生活 shēnghuó	student 学生 xuéshēng
vivid 生动 shēngdòng	

Ancient character

Compound element

crops

noun

adjective

年

year; age; a period in one's life; a period in history; harvest; New Year

annual; yearly

Compound element

Note in Chinese

年 = 𥝊

这个字取自于谷穗的形状，左上的一撇表示饱满的谷穗垂向土地。北方的粮食作物是一年一收，所以是"年"。

⬤ **READ ALOUD**

Once a YEAR, when wheat is ready to be harvested, it bows its head towards the earth. YEAR is nián（年）.

Stroke order

Composite capabilities: 1 2 3 4 5 6 7 8 9 10

prefix/phrase	suffix/phrase
age 年龄 niánlíng	teenager 少年 shàonián
grade 年级 niánjí	youngster 青年 qīngnián
young 年轻 niánqīng	New Year 新年 xīnnián
aged 年老 niánlǎo	celebrating New Year 过年 guònián
years 年代 niándài	next year 明年 míngnián

Ancient character

Compound element

了 finish

verb
adverb
auxiliary word

liǎo: *finish; end;
accomplished;
at the last;
know clearly;*
le: *entirely;
completely*

Compound element

Note in Chinese

了 = ㇗

这个字象征着一个孩子已经有了站立的能力；后作为虚词有两个功能：表示在过去、现在或未来行为的"完成"；表示事物在时空状态上的"改变"。

🔊 **READ ALOUD**

This baby's time inside his mother's womb IS OVER. His own life has begun. IS OVER is le（了）.

Stroke order

Composite capabilities: 1 2 3 4 5 6 7 8 9 10

prefix/phrase	suffix/phrase
understand 了解 liǎojiě	drunk tea 喝了茶 hēle chá
finish 了结 liǎojié	studied Chinese 学中文了
know clearly 了然 liǎorán	xué Zhōngwén le
wonderful 了不得 liǎobudé	come in soon 快来了 kuài lái le

Ancient
character

Compound element

习 feather

| verb
noun | 习 | practise;
be used to

habit; custom |

Compound element

Note in Chinese

习

这是"習"的简
体。字像一只雏鸟
张翅往下飞。

🔊 READ ALOUD

This baby bird has to PRACTISE facing the right way up before he can
head for the sun! PRACTISE is xí（习）.

Stroke order

Composite capabilities: 1 2 3 4 5 6 7 8 9 10

prefix/phrase	suffix/phrase
custom 习惯 xíguàn	learn 学习 xuéxí
exercises 习题 xítí	practise 练习 liànxí
habits and characteristics 习性 xíxìng	exercise one's kill in 实习 shíxí
drawings/works 习作 xízuò	reviewing 复习 fùxí
	military exercises 演习 yǎnxí

Ancient character

verb;
adjective

fly; flit; flutter

Compound element

飞 *fly*

Compound element

Note in Chinese

飞 = 飞

这是"飛"的简体。

🔊 READ ALOUD

Birds have to flap their wings in order to FLY. FLY is fēi（飞）.

Stroke order

Composite capabilities: 1 2 3 4 5 6 7 8 9 10

prefix/phrase	suffix/phrase
aircraft 飞机 fēijī	take off 起飞 qǐfēi
fly to 飞往 fēiwǎng	fly non-stop 直飞 zhífēi
swift 飞快 fēikuài	
flying bird 飞鸟 fēiniǎo	

Ancient
character

Compound element

⊘ blinded eye

noun
adjective

the people;
the masses

person of

folk

Note in Chinese

民 = ⊘ + ╀
上面是一只没有眼
珠的眼睛，下面的
部分代表人的身
体。意思是盲目。

Compound element

╀ body

-- 🔊 **READ ALOUD** -

Without education, the common PEOPLE risk being blind to the truth.
PEOPLE is mín（民）.

Stroke order

Composite capabilities: 1 2 3 4 5 6 7 8 9 10

prefix/phrase	suffix/phrase
democracy 民主 mínzhǔ	the masses 人民 rénmín
the people's livelihood	citizen 公民 gōngmín
民生 mínshēng	city residents 市民 shìmín
be run by the community	the people of nation 国民 guómín
民办 mínbàn	
civil 民用 mínyòng	

Ancient character

Compound element

一 second

verb

买

buy; purchase

Compound element

头 head

Note in Chinese

买 = 一 + 头

这是"買"的简体。上面的"一"是一个容器，下面的"头"（P2头）表示计算。

🔊 **READ ALOUD**

When BUYING, most people try to reduce the price by bargaining with the vendor. BUYING is mǎi（买）.

Stroke order

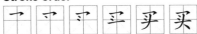

Composite capabilities: 1 2 3 4 5 6 7 8 9 10

prefix/phrase	suffix/phrase
shopping 买东西 mǎi dōngxi	easy to buy 好买 hǎomǎi
business 买卖 mǎimài	difficult to buy 难买 nánmǎi
the buying party 买方 mǎifāng	
pay the bill 买单 mǎidān	

Ancient character

Compound element

 temple

noun

京

the capital of a country

the abbreviated form of Beijing

Compound element

 city gate

Note in Chinese

京 = 合 + 爪

字的上部是建造在高处的庙宇，下面是城墙的部分。

🔊 READ ALOUD

A temple sitting on top of a city wall usually denotes a gateway to the CAPITAL. CAPITAL is jīng（京）.

Stroke order

Composite capabilities: 1 2 3 4 5 6 7 8 9 10

prefix/phrase	suffix/phrase
capital city 京城 jīngchéng	Beijing 北京 Běijīng
Beijing opera 京剧 Jīngjù	Nanjing 南京 Nánjīng
of special Beijing flavour 京味儿 jīngwèir	leave the capital 离京(Beijing) lí Jīng

Ancient
character

Compound element
亠 roof
口 window

| adjective | 高 | tall;
high;
loud |

Note in Chinese

高=亠+口+冂+口
这是一个两层都有窗
子的高大的建筑。

Compound element
冂 hall
口 window

🔊 **READ ALOUD**

A TALL building usually has windows on both floors. TALL is gāo（高）.

Stroke order

`丶` `亠` `市` `市` `肻` `肻` `高` `高` `高` `高`

Composite capabilities: 1 2 3 4 5 6 7 8 9 10

prefix/phrase	suffix/phrase
superb 高超 gāochāo	climb hills 登高 dēnggāo
tall and big 高大 gāodà	
brilliant 高明 gāomíng	
happy 高兴 gāoxìng	

Ancient character

Compound element
⼇ = lid
亠

verb

离

*leave; depart;
keep away;
be away
from; without;
independent of*

Note in Chinese

离 = 亠 + 禸

这是"離"的简体。
上面是屋顶。下面的
结构里出现"×"，
这个符号时有警告的
含义。最下的部分也
有"陷阱"的意思。

Compound element
× + 凵 =
warning + open
box
禸 trap

🌀 READ ALOUD

LEAVE quickly, there is a dangerous trap inside this building! LEAVE is
lí（离）.

Stroke order

Composite capabilities: 1 2 3 4 5 6 7 8 9 10

prefix/phrase	suffix/phrase
depart 离开 líkāi	keep away from 远离 yuǎnlí
odd 离奇 líqí	leave 分离 fēnlí
retire 离休 líxiū	distance 距离 jùlí

Ancient
character

noun
adjective
verb

Compound element
冫 icicles

冰

Compound element
水   river

Note in Chinese

冰 = 仌 + 氺

左边是冰凌，右边
是水（P240水），
表示水已结冰。

ice
feel cold
put ice around

🔊 READ ALOUD

When water freezes it turns to ICE. ICE is bīng（冰）.

Stroke order

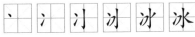

Composite capabilities: 1 2 3 4 5 **6** 7 8 9 10

prefix/phrase	suffix/phrase
iceberg 冰山 bīngshān	skating 滑冰 huábīng
ice cold 冰冷 bīnglěng	
ice water 冰水 bīngshuǐ	
glacier 冰河 bīnghé	

Ancient
character

verb
noun
measure word

Compound element
讠（言）*words/
language*

记

Compound element
己 *oneself*

remember;
write down

notes; mark;
sign

Note in Chinese

记 = 言 + 己

这是"記"的简体。
左边是语言，右边是
自己（P161己）。

🍎 **READ ALOUD**

Taking notes in her own language can sometimes help a foreign student
REMEMBER what was spoken at a lecture. REMEMBER is jì（记）.

Stroke order

Composite capabilities: 1 2 3 4 5 6 7 8 9 10

prefix/phrase	suffix/phrase
remember 记得 jìde	diary 日记 rìjì
notes 记录 jìlù	notes 笔记 bǐjì
memory 记性 jìxing	travel notes 游记 yóujì
reporter 记者 jìzhě	a slap in the face 一记耳光
learn by heart 记住 jìzhù	yí jì ěrguāng

Ancient character

verb
noun

Compound element

讠（言）
language/speak

议

Compound element

义 *justice*

Note in Chinese

议 = 讠+ 义

这是 " 議 " 的简体。左边是用来沟通的语言，右边是正义（P1义）。

discuss;
exchange views on;
talk over
opinion; view

🔊 READ ALOUD

The best DISCUSSIONS aim to arrive at a fair and equitable result for all concerned. DISCUSS is yì（议）.

Stroke order

Composite capabilities: 1 2 3 4 5 6 7 8 9 10

prefix/phrase	suffix/phrase
topic of discussion 议题 yìtí	meeting 会议 huìyì
parliament 议会 yìhuì	objection 异议 yìyì
speaker 议长 yìzhǎng	
agree on 议定 yìdìng	

Ancient
character

verb
noun

Compound element
讠（言）
speaking

识

Compound element
只 *only*

Note in Chinese

识 ＝ 讠 ＋ 只

这是"識"的简体。
左边是语言，右边是
"只"。

know
knowledge

🍴 READ ALOUD

Words alone without the backing of real KNOWLEDGE are like bubbles
without substance. KNOWLEDGE is shí（识）.

Stroke order

Composite capabilities: 1 **2** 3 4 5 6 7 8 9 10

prefix/phrase	suffix/phrase
learn to read 识字 shízì	recognise 认识 rènshi
distinguish 识别 shíbié	knowledge 知识 zhīshi
penetrate 识破 shípò	sensibleness 见识 jiànshi
	known each other 相识 xiāngshí

Ancient character

verb

Compound element
讠（言）
speak/ language

诉

Compound element
斥
upbraid/exclude

tell; accuse; appeal to

Note in Chinese

诉 = 讠 + 斥

这是"訴"的简体。这个字一边是语言，另一边是一把锋利的斧头。在法庭上是没有戏言的。

🔊 READ ALOUD

To make an ACCUSE in court, a barrister has to be very clever with words. ACCUSE is sù（诉）.

Stroke order

Composite capabilities: 1 2 3 4 5 6 7 8 9 10

prefix/phrase	suffix/phrase
lawsuit 诉讼 sùsòng	tell 告诉 gàosu
tell 诉说 sùshuō	appeal to 上诉 shàngsù
complain 诉苦 sùkǔ	

Ancient character

noun
verb

Compound element
讠（言）
language/ words

话

Compound element
舌（千+口）
tongue (arrow + mouth)

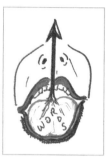

Note in Chinese

话 = 言 + 舌

这是"话"的简体。左边是语言，右边的下面是口，口上是一套弓箭。

word; talk

talk about; speak about

READ ALOUD

SPEECH can sometimes wound more than a weapon! SPEECH is huà（话）.

Stroke order

Composite capabilities: 1 2 3 4 5 6 7 8 9 10

prefix/phrase	suffix/phrase
talking topic 话题 huàtí	speak 说话 shuōhuà
stage ply 话剧 huàjù	Mandarin 普通话 Pǔtōnghuà
words 话语 huàyǔ	Shanghai dialogue 上海话 Shànghǎihuà
implication 话音 huàyīn	tell the truth 说真话 shuō zhēnhuà

Ancient
character

	verb noun	
Compound element 讠（言） *speak/ language*	说	Compound element 兑 *exchange*
	speak; talk; say; explain; scold theory	

Note in Chinese

说 = 訁 + 兑

这是"說"的简
体。左边是语言，
右边是"兑"：交
换。组合后表达用
语言沟通。

READ ALOUD

To SPEAK with others is to exchange information with them. SPEAK is
shuō（说）.

Stroke order

Composite capabilities: 1 2 3 4 5 6 7 8 9 10

prefix/phrase	suffix/phrase
speak 说话 shuōhuà	doctrine 学说 xuéshuō
explain 说明 shuōmíng	novel 小说 xiǎoshuō
argue 说理 shuōlǐ	nonsense 胡说 húshuō
stand by one's word 说一不二 shuōyībú'èr	

Ancient
character

noun
verb

Compound element		Compound element
讠（言）*language/speak*	语	吾 *five + sense= oneself*

Note in Chinese

语 =

"語"的简体。这
个字左边是说话，
右边是一个独立的
字"吾"："五"
在上面，"口"在
下面，表示人的
"五种感觉"。

language; words;
tongue

speak; say

── 🔊 **READ ALOUD** ──

If five people talk in different LANGUAGES at the same time, nobody will
understand them! LANGUAGE is yǔ（语）.

Stroke order

Composite capabilities: 1 2 3 4 5 6 7 8 9 10

prefix/phrase	suffix/phrase
language 语言 yǔyán	English 英语 Yīngyǔ
manner of speaking 语气 yǔqì	Japanese 日语 Rìyǔ
grammar 语法 yǔfǎ	German 德语 Déyǔ
language and literature 语文 yǔwén	French 法语 Fǎyǔ
families of languages 语种 yǔzhǒng	

Ancient character

verb

Compound element

讠（言）*speak/ communicate*

读

Compound element

卖 *sell*

read;
read aloud;
attend school;
study

Note in Chinese

读 = 言 + 卖

这是"讀"的简体。左边是语言，右边是卖（P43卖）出。

─ ✸ **READ ALOUD** ─

To sell one's ideas to an audience, sometimes it is good to READ ALOUD from a prepared document. READ ALOUD is dú（读）.

Stroke order

丶 讠 订 汁 读 读 读 读 读 读

Composite capabilities: 1 2 3 4 5 6 7 8 9 10

prefix/phrase	suffix/phrase
reader 读者 dúzhě	read out 朗读 lǎngdú
attend school 读书 dúshū	

Ancient character

verb

↑

Compound element
讠（言）
language

← 请 →

Compound element
青 *young/energy /nice/green*

↓

please; invite; request; ask

Note in Chinese

请 = 讠 + 青

这是"請"的简体。左边是语言，右边是"青"，"青"字像是一棵干粗叶茂的树。凡有"青"做组件的字，都含有活力与美好的意思。

READ ALOUD

It is polite to say PLEASE before any request in order to engender good, pure energy between people. PLEASE is qǐng（请）.

Stroke order

Composite capabilities: 1 2 3 4 5 6 7 8 9 10

prefix/phrase	suffix/phrase
may I ask/excuse me 请问 qǐngwèn	invite respectfully 敬请 jìngqǐng
invite someone to dinner 请客 qǐngkè	entertain to dinner 宴请 yànqǐng
please come in 请进 qǐngjìn	
request 请求 qǐngqiú	

Ancient
character

```
          ┌─────────────┐
          │    verb     │
          └─────────────┘
                ▲
┌──────────────┐      ┌──────────────────┐
│ Compound element │  │ Compound element │
│   讠（言）    │  谢  │    身 + 寸       │
│   language    │ ◄─►  │  body + measure  │
│     [seal]    │      │   [seal]+[seal]  │
└──────────────┘      └──────────────────┘
                ▼
          ┌─────────────────┐
          │ thank; make an  │
          │   apology       │
          │                 │
          │ decline; wither │
          └─────────────────┘
```

Note in Chinese

谢 = 言 + 身 + 寸

"謝"的简体。这
个字的左边是语
言，中间是身体，
右边是尺度。言谢
时肢体语言也要求
适度。

🔊 READ ALOUD

When we say THANK YOU, we not only use words but also a well-judged
bow. THANK is xiè（谢）.

Stroke order

丶	讠	讠	讠	讠	讠	讠	谢	谢	谢

谢	谢

Composite capabilities: 1 2 3 4 5 6 7 8 9 10

prefix/phrase	suffix/phrase
thank you 谢谢你 xièxie nǐ	thank 感谢 gǎnxiè
gratitude 谢意 xièyì	express thanks 致谢 zhìxiè
thank goodness 谢天谢地 xiètiānxièdì	say thanks in person 面谢 miànxiè

Ancient
character

Compound element
十 + 一
ten + second

sell

verb ← 卖 → sell; betray;
exert to the
utmost;
show off

Compound element
头 head

Note in Chinese

卖 = 十 + 一 + 头
这是"賣"的简
体。与"买"（P28
买）字比较，只是
在"一"的顶上加
一个"十"。

🔊 READ ALOUD

When vendors buy and SELL, they try to make at least a 10% profit. SELL
is mài（卖）.

Stroke order

      一 十 韦 韦 韦 韦 卖 卖

Composite capabilities: 1 2 3 4 5 6 7 8 9 10

prefix/phrase	suffix/phrase
selling products 卖东西 mài dōngxi	business 买卖 mǎimài
sell property 卖房 mài fáng	a sale goods for charity 义卖 yìmài
exert all one's strength 卖力 màilì	

Ancient
character

Compound element
米 a tree at the
top of mountain

noun

南

south

Compound element
羊 trees

Note in Chinese

南 = 米 + 羊

山顶上是树，山坡
上也是树。在中
国，树木繁茂的一
面一定是面向阳光
的"南"面。

READ ALOUD

Forests tend to grow on the SOUTH slopes of mountains where they get
the most sun. SOUTH is nán（南）.

Stroke order

Composite capabilities: 1 2 3 4 5 6 7 8 9 10

prefix/phrase	suffix/phrase
southern side 南边 nánbiān	facing south 朝南 cháo nán
South China Sea 南海 Nánhǎi	Vietnam 越南 Yuènán
south wind 南风 nánfēng	
pumpkin 南瓜 nánguā	

Ancient
character

Compound element

厂 cliff

verb adjective adverb noun	历	go through; experience all previous covering all calendar

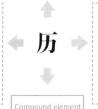

Compound element

力 strength

ϡ

Note in Chinese

历 = 厂 + ϡ

这是"歷"的简
体。字由左上的石
壁悬崖与右下的发
"力"（P89力）组
成。可能要表达一
个难忘的经历。

READ ALOUD

Both strength and EXPERIENCE are necessary qualities for a serious
mountaineer. EXPERIENCE is lì（历）.

Stroke order

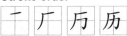

Composite capabilities: 1 2 3 4 5 6 7 8 9 10

prefix/phrase	suffix/phrase
history 历史 lìshǐ	experience 经历 jīnglì
over the years 历年 lìnián	calendar 日历 rìlì
come clearly into view 历历在目 lìlìzàimù	

Ancient
character

verb
noun

Compound element
匸 *an one side opened space/a hiding place*

医

Compound element

矢 *arrow*

cure; treat

doctor;
medical science

Note in Chinese

医 = 匸 + 矢

这 是 "醫" 的 简
体。在 一 个 右 边 敞
开 居 所 "匸" 里 有
一 支 箭 "矢"。表
示 这 个 地 方 是 医
院。

READ ALOUD

In ancient times, practising MEDICINE often involved extracting arrows
from wounded soldiers on the battlefield. MEDICINE is yī（医）.

Stroke order

Composite capabilities: 1 2 3 4 5 6 7 8 9 10

prefix/phrase	suffix/phrase
medical doctor 医生 yīshēng	traditional Chinese medical science
hospital 医院 yīyuàn	中医 zhōngyī
medical science 医学 yīxué	western medical science 西医 xīyī

Ancient character

verb
preposition
adjective

Note in Chinese

到 = 𡆥 + 刂

字的左边是一只头朝下的鸟飞回它的窝；右边是一个人形。组合后表示人到达一个预定的目标，如同鸟回到鸟巢。

Compound element

至 *arrive*

 a bird is heading to the net

到

Compound element

刂 *person*

彳

arrive; reach; go to

up to; up until

thoughtful

🐦 **READ ALOUD**

A person ARRIVING home is like a bird returning to its nest. ARRIVE is dào（到）.

Stroke order

Composite capabilities: 1 2 3 4 5 6 7 8 9 10

prefix/phrase	suffix/phrase
arrive 到达 dàodá	thoughtful 周到 zhōudào
properly 到位 dàowèi	been done 做到 zuòdào

Ancient character

Compound element

冂 an opened container

noun ← **内** → inside; with; inner part; in; internal; one's wife

Note in Chinese

内 = 冂 + 人

这个字是由一个封闭的容器和一个头在外面、身体在容器里面的人组成的。

Compound element

人 person

🎧 READ ALOUD

This Japanese man is enjoying a soak INSIDE his bathtub. INSIDE is nèi (内).

Stroke order

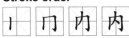

Composite capabilities: 1 2 3 4 5 6 7 8 9 10

prefix/phrase	suffix/phrase
content 内容 nèiróng	internal 对内 duìnèi
heat 内心 nèixīn	inside of the school camp 校内
underwear 内衣 nèiyī	xiàonèi

Ancient
character

verb
noun
preposition

Compound element

 furniture

用

Compound element

Note in Chinese

用 =

字形是一个放杂物
的架子。

use; need;
eat; drink

expenses;
usefulness

with

🔊 **READ ALOUD**

A low stand with six partitions can be very USEFUL! USE is yòng（用）.

Stroke order

    用

Composite capabilities: 1 2 3 4 5 6 7 8 9 10

prefix/phrase	suffix/phrase
usage 用法 yòngfǎ	useful 有用 yǒuyòng
please drink tea 用茶 yòngchá	use 使用 shǐyòng
exert oneself 用力 yònglì	no need 不用 búyòng
choose a person for a job 用人 yòngrén	

Ancient
character

Compound element

彐 join

adjective
verb
adverb
conjunction

同

same; alike;
similar;
be the same as

together

with; and

Note in Chinese

同 = 彐 + 廿

字形为两个人手拉
着手，下面是资
源。

Compound element

口 mouth

廿

🔊 READ ALOUD

Sharing resources and working TOGETHER produces the best results.
TOGETHER is tóng（同）.

Stroke order

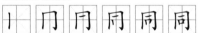

Composite capabilities: 1 2 3 4 5 6 7 8 9 10

prefix/phrase	suffix/phrase
fellow student 同学 tóngxué	the same 相同 xiāngtóng
at the same time 同时 tóngshí	not the same 不同 bùtóng
colleague 同事 tóngshì	harmonization 大同 dàtóng
go the same way 同路 tónglù	

Ancient character

Compound element

| | frame

noun
verb

网

net; network; Internet

catch with net

Note in Chinese

网 = ||+X

这是"網"的简体。外面是框架，里面是交织的线绳。

Compound element

XX net

🔊 READ ALOUD

The NET used in football consists of a frame and crisscrossing strings. NET is wǎng (网).

Stroke order

丨 冂 冂 冈 网 网

Composite capabilities: 1 2 3 4 5 6 7 8 9 10

prefix/phrase	suffix/phrase
tennis 网球 wǎngqiú	get internet 上网 shàngwǎng
website 网站 wǎngzhàn	net of ball games 球网 qiúwǎng
cyber friend 网友 wǎngyǒu	fishnet 渔网 yúwǎng

Ancient
character

Compound element

) (eight

Note in Chinese

八 =) (

这个字像两撇胡须。

numeral

八

eight

Compound element

🔊 **READ ALOUD**

A Chinese moustache looks like the number EIGHT. EIGHT is bā（八）.

Stroke order

Composite capabilities: 1 2 3 4 **5** 6 7 8 9 10

prefix/phrase	suffix/phrase
all directions 八方 bāfāng	bits and pieces 七七八八 qīqībābā
80% 八成 bāchéng	

Ancient
character

Compound element
八
eight/separate

verb
noun
measure word

分

divide
branch

Note in Chinese

分 =)(+ 丿

字的下边是一把长
柄的刀，这把刀正
在把上面的东西切
分开来。

Compound element
刀 knife

🎵 READ ALOUD

A knife can be used to DIVIDE an aubergine into two pieces. DIVIDE is
fēn（分）.

Stroke order

Composite capabilities: 1 2 3 4 5 6 7 8 9 10

prefix/phrase	suffix/phrase
separate 分开 fēnkāi	score 得分 défēn
say good bye 分手 fēnshǒu	two third 三分之二 sān fēnzhī èr
mark 分数 fēnshù	five pennies 五分钱 wǔfēn qián

Ancient
character

Compound element

八 eight/divide

adjective
noun
verb

公

public; general;
common;
equitable

official
make public

Note in Chinese

公 = 八 + ㄙ

字的下部是一个钱
袋，上面是两只把
钱袋打开的手。

Compound element

ㄙ
private object

🔊 READ ALOUD

To share one's possessions is to be PUBLIC–spirited. PUBLIC is
gōng（公）.

Stroke order

Composite capabilities: 1 2 3 4 5 6 7 8 9 10

prefix/phrase	suffix/phrase
fair 公平 gōngpíng	offer as a tribute 奉公 fèng gōng
open 公开 gōngkāi	
public 公共 gōnggòng	
husband's father 公公 gōnggong	

Ancient
character

Compound element

  divide

*numeral
adjective
adverb*

半

*half
very little
partly*

Compound element

an ox

Note in Chinese

半 = 八 + 㐅

这个古字像是半个
羊（P267羊）头与
半个牛（P221牛）
头合在了一起。

🎧 **READ ALOUD**

This character is completely symmetrical. Each HALF is a mirror image of
the other. HALF is bàn（半）.

Stroke order

Composite capabilities: 1 2 3 4 5 6 7 8 9 10

prefix/phrase	suffix/phrase
half a day 半天 bàntiān	a half 一半 yíbàn
on the way 半路 bànlù	
half a year 半年 bànnián	

Ancient character

Compound element

arms & hands

adjective
verb
advert

共

common;
general

share

together

Compound element

arms & hands

Note in Chinese

共 = 𠬞 + 𠬞

上下一共四只手挽
在一起。表示共识
与共事。

🎧 READ ALOUD

Many hands work together to create a COMMON good. COMMON is gòng（共）.

Stroke order

Composite capabilities: 1 2 3 4 **5** 6 7 8 9 10

prefix/phrase	suffix/phrase
shared 共同 gòngtóng	public 公共 gōnggòng
common understanding 共识 gòngshí	in total 一共 yígòng
republic 共和 gònghé	
share 共用 gòngyòng	

Ancient
character

Compound element

hands with rope

verb

noun

关

close; shut

mountain pass

Compound element

Note in Chinese

关=

这 是 " 關 " 的 简
体 。 两 只 大 手 把 门
闩 好 、 关 严 。

READ ALOUD

Heavy doors have to be SHUT properly with both hands. SHUT is
guān（关）.

Stroke order

Composite capabilities: 1 2 3 4 5 6 7 8 9 10

prefix/phrase	suffix/phrase
be concern about 关心 guānxīn	customs 海关 hǎiguān
relations 关系 guānxi	public relations 公关 gōngguān
pay close attention to 关注 guānzhù	

Ancient character

Compound element
ソ head
人 body

noun

弟

younger brother

Compound element
弓 a rope-shaped object

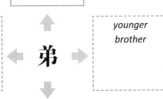

Note in Chinese

弟 = 𠃊 + 弓

这个字中有一个
"弓"形，是表示
顺着中间的柱子从
下而上，次第旋
升。

🔊 READ ALOUD

The two snakes coiled round the tree trunk are my YOUNGER BROTHERS.
YOUNGER BROTHERS is dì（弟）.

Stroke order

Composite capabilities: 1 2 3 4 5 6 7 8 9 10

prefix/phrase	suffix/phrase
younger brother 弟弟 dìdi	younger male cousin 表弟 biǎodì
	brothers 兄弟 xiōngdì

Ancient
character

Compound element

ᵛᵛ handles

ᵞ

Note in Chinese

单 = ᵞ + 甲

这是"單"的简
体。字形是一辆有
两个把手的单轮
车。

adjective
adverb
noun

单

single; one;
thin; simple

only; alone

sheet; bill

Compound element

車 wheel

甲

🕮 **READ ALOUD**

A wheelbarrow has a SINGLE wheel and two handles. SINGLE is
dān（单）.

Stroke order

Composite capabilities: 1 2 3 4 5 6 7 8 9 10

prefix/phrase	suffix/phrase
single 单身 dānshēn	simple 简单 jiǎndān
single person 单人 dānrén	alone 单单 dāndān
	menu 菜单 càidān

Ancient character

Compound element

介 ways

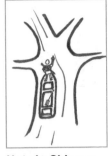

noun
adjective

前

front; forward; ago; before; first

proceeding; former; future

Note in Chinese

前 = 介 + ⏶ + ⊨

字的上部是脚，左下是船，右下是河道。船在河中，人置足船头，顺水前行。

Compound element

⏶ + ⊨
foot + boat

🎵 READ ALOUD

A man stands at the FRONT of his boat in order to guide it forwards. FRONT is qián（前）.

Stroke order

Composite capabilities: 1 2 3 4 5 6 7 8 9 **10**

prefix/phrase	suffix/phrase
in front 前边 qiánbiān	at present 目前 mùqián
the year before last 前年 qiánnián	in front of eye 眼前 yǎnqián
forefathers 前人 qiánrén	before the event 事前 shìqián
cause and effect 前因后果 qiányīnhòuguǒ	prehistoric 史前 shǐqián

Ancient character

Compound element

 hairs

noun
adjective

measure word

首

head; leader; chief

first

Note in Chinese

首 = ⺍ + 𦣻

字的上边是头发，下边是面孔，所以是头部，文言文称为"首"。

Compound element

face

READ ALOUD

A human HEAD usually comprises of a face and some hair. HEAD is shǒu（首）.

Stroke order

Composite capabilities: 1 2 3 4 5 6 7 8 9 10

prefix/phrase	suffix/phrase
capital 首都 shǒudū	old age 白首 báishǒu
the first place 首位 shǒuwèi	behead 斩首 zhǎnshǒu
before all others 首先 shǒuxiān	

Ancient character

Compound element
真 true/real

adjective
adverb

真

true; real; clear

really; truly;
indeed

Compound element

Note in Chinese

真 = 鼑

这个字的原形是一
个放在火上烧的容
器，里面是被煮沸
的物件。这可能是
古代作为鉴别真伪
的一种方法。

🔊 READ ALOUD

Some people believe that TRUTH comes to us from heaven above. TRUE is zhēn（真）.

Stroke order

| | | | | | | | | | |
|一|十|𠂇|亩|亩|亩|直|直|真|真|

Composite capabilities: 1 2 3 4 5 6 7 8 9 10

prefix/phrase	suffix/phrase
truth 真理 zhēnlǐ	naive 天真 tiānzhēn
vacuum 真空 zhēnkōng	
the real situation 真相 zhēnxiàng	
whole-hearted 真心 zhēnxīn	

Ancient
character

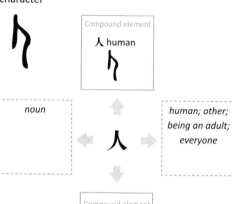

Compound element

人 human

noun

人

*human; other;
being an adult;
everyone*

Compound element

Note in Chinese

人 = 亻

甲骨文的"人"是
一个在劳作中的形
态。

🎵 **READ ALOUD**

PEOPLE are always rushing around, seldom stopping to smell the roses.
PEOPLE is rén（人）.

Stroke order

Composite capabilities: 1 2 3 4 5 6 7 8 9 10

prefix/phrase	suffix/phrase
the people 人民 rénmín	man 男人 nánrén
ethnic 人种 rénzhǒng	woman 女人 nǚrén
humanity 人道 réndào	adult 大人 dàrén
talent 人才 réncái	skilled man 能人 néngrén
life 人生 rénshēng	immoral people 小人 xiǎorén

Ancient
character

Compound element
▲ mouth and tongue

noun		today; modern; now; present

今

Compound element
▬ wine

Note in Chinese

今 = ▲ + ▬

上边的部分是一个
向下张开的口与口
中的舌头，下面一
横代表酒。表示当
下、现今的意思。

🔊 **READ ALOUD**

The cuckoo clock woke me up at 8:35am. TODAY. TODAY is jīn（今）.

Stroke order

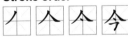

Composite capabilities: 1 2 3 4 5 6 7 8 9 10

prefix/phrase	suffix/phrase
today 今天 jīntiān	from now 从今 cóngjīn
from now on 今后 jīnhòu	at the present 如今 rújīn
this year 今年 jīnnián	
this life 今生 jīnshēng	

Ancient character

verb

noun

Compound element
人 two mouths

会

Compound element
云 cloud

Note in Chinese

会 = ⊖ + ♂

这是"會"的简体。人多得像云朵，所以是聚会。

meet; get together; know; can; be able to; be good at; be likely to; pay

meeting; society; capital; a moment

─ 🔊 READ ALOUD ─

When two rain clouds MEET, there is potential for a downpour. MEET is huì（会）.

Stroke order

丿 人 人 今 会 会

Composite capabilities: 1 2 3 4 5 6 7 8 9 10

prefix/phrase	suffix/phrase
meet with 会见 huìjiàn	parliament 议会 yìhuì
meeting 会议 huìyì	evening party 晚会 wǎnhuì
receive a guest 会客 huìkè	hold or attend a meeting 开会 kāihuì
conversation 会话 huìhuà	
I will go 我会去 wǒ huì qù	mastered 学会 xuéhuì
I can swim 我会游泳 wǒ huì yóuyǒng	a moment 一会儿 yíhuìr

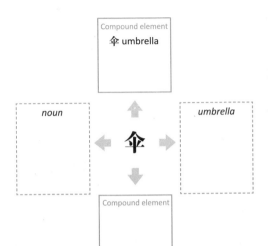

Compound element
伞 umbrella

noun

伞

umbrella

Compound element

Note in Chinese

伞

这是"伞"的简体。"伞"的字形与真伞相差无几。

⚫ READ ALOUD

This character looks just like an UMBRELLA. UMBRELLA is sǎn (伞).

Stroke order

Composite capabilities: 1 2 3 4 5 6 7 8 9 10

prefix/phrase	suffix/phrase
paratrooper 伞兵 sǎnbīng	use umbrella 打伞 dǎsǎn
	parasol 阳伞 yángsǎn
	umbrella 雨伞 yǔsǎn

Ancient character

verb

noun

Compound element

亻

alive people

化

Compound element

匕

dead people

change; turn; convert; melt; digest; burn up

chemistry

Note in Chinese

化 = 亻 + 匕

左右两边各表示是一个人：头向上是生，头向下是死，万物都在遵循这个变化。

🔊 **READ ALOUD**

Energy reaches upwards when we are alive, downwards when we die. Constant CHANGE from one form to another is the law of nature. CHANGE is huà（化）.

Stroke order

Composite capabilities: 1 2 3 4 5 6 7 8 9 10

prefix/phrase	suffix/phrase
chemistry 化学 huàxué	change 变化 biànhuà
fossil 化石 huàshí	nationalisation 国有化 guóyǒuhuà
ease off 化解 huàjiě	

Ancient
character

plural

Compound element
亻 *people*

们

Compound element
门 *gate/door*

Note in Chinese

们 = 亻 + 門

这是"們"的简体。
"门"是家庭出入的
必经之处，以"人"
（P63人）和"门"
（P110门）组合，体
现多于一个人。

we; you; they;
ours; yours...

READ ALOUD

SEVERAL PEOPLE live behind these doors. PLURAL FOR MANKIND is
men（们）.

Stroke order

Composite capabilities: 1 2 3 4 5 6 7 8 9 10

prefix/phrase	suffix/phrase
	we 我们 wǒmen
	you(plural) 你们 nǐmen
	they 他们/她们 tāmen
	students 学生们 xuéshengmen

Ancient
character

conjunction
adverb

Compound element
亻(人) people

但

Compound element
旦 sunrise

but; still;
nevertheless

only; merely

but ...

Note in Chinese

但 = 亻 + 旦

左边是人，右边的
"旦"是早上的太
阳。最先的"但"
含袒露之意，后做
连词使用，已经与
太阳无关。

🎵 READ ALOUD

The sun has risen over the horizon BUT this man has no work to go to.
BUT is dàn（但）.

Stroke order

Composite capabilities: 1 2 3 4 5 6 7 8 9 10

prefix/phrase	suffix/phrase
but 但是 dànshì	not only 不但 búdàn
If only 但愿 dànyuàn	

Ancient character

pronoun

Compound element

亻(人) *people*

你

Compound element

尔 *arrows/ you*

you

Note in Chinese

你 = 亻 + 尔

左是人，右是数箭在弦。蛮荒时代，除了自己，别人都可能是敌人。因此问明来历的同时，箭羽相对。古字本为"尔"，加"人"偏旁是后起字，大约始于隋朝。

🔊 READ ALOUD

Three arrows have been aimed at your heart. YOU must be very popular with Cupid! YOU is nǐ（你）.

Stroke order

Composite capabilities: 1 2 3 4 5 6 7 8 9 10

prefix/phrase	suffix/phrase
hello 你好 nǐ hǎo	
you (plural)你们 nǐmen	
life-and-death 你死我活 nǐsǐwǒhuó	

Ancient
character

Note in Chinese

体 = 人 + 本

这是"體"的简体。
人在左，"本"
（P193本）字在右，
取 "人之根本是身
体"的意思。形象
的解释可为：远古
人栖居在树上，以
防野兽伤身，所以
人与树木是一体。

noun
verb

Compound element

亻（人）*man*

体

Compound element

本 *base/root*

body; style;
system;

personally to
do... ; put oneself
in...

🐾 READ ALOUD

Human BODIES were soft and vulnerable to wild beasts so they sometimes lived on top of trees for protection. BODY is tǐ（体）.

Stroke order

Composite capabilities: 1 2 3 4 5 6 7 8 9 10

prefix/phrase	suffix/phrase
sports 体育 tǐyù	body 身体 shēntǐ
physical strength 体力 tǐlì	the upper part of the body 上体
indicate 体现 tǐxiàn	shàngtǐ
feel from experience 体会 tǐhuì	

Ancient character

noun
measure word

Compound element

亻（人）
people

位

立 *stand*

position; place; location

digit

Note in Chinese

位 = 亻 + 企

左边是人，右边是
站立的"立"（P242
立），组合后表示
人立于世的位置。

🎧 **READ ALOUD**

In a healthy society there is a PLACE for everyone. Vive la difference!
PLACE is wèi（位）.

Stroke order

丿 亻 亻 仁 仿 位 位

Composite capabilities: 1 2 3 4 5 6 7 8 9 10

prefix/phrase	suffix/phrase
position 位置 wèizhì	social status 地位 dìwèi
seat 位子 wèizi	water position 水位 shuǐwèi
be located 位于 wèiyú	one guest 一位客人 yí wèi kèrén

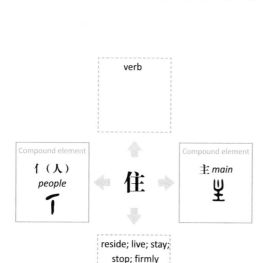

Note in Chinese

住 = 亻 + 业

左边是人，右边是
"主"（P3 主）：
一个便于上下联
络、布局合理的工
程结构，其组合表
示人栖居或停留。

🍀 READ ALOUD

One of the main needs for man is to have somewhere to LIVE. LIVE is zhù（住）.

Stroke order

Composite capabilities: 1 2 3 4 5 6 7 8 9 10

prefix/phrase	suffix/phrase
housing 住房 zhùfáng	stop 停住 tíngzhù
board at school 住校 zhùxiào	halt 站住 zhànzhù
address 住址 zhùzhǐ	
shut up 住口 zhùkǒu	

Ancient
character

verb
noun

Compound element

亻（人）
man/person

使

Compound element

吏
civil servant

diplomat; envoy;
messenger

use; make; send;
cause

Note in Chinese

使 = 亻 + 吏

左边是人，右上
是公事，右下是
"手"；三部分组
合表示"口令、公
务、职责"，即使
命。

READ ALOUD

A DIPLOMAT requires a good head, an efficient pair of hands, and above all, a human heart. DIPLOMAT is shǐ（使）.

Stroke order

丿　亻　仁　仁　侗　侗　使　使

Composite capabilities: 1 2 **3** 4 5 6 7 8 9 10

prefix/phrase	suffix/phrase
envoy 使节 shǐjié	ambassador 大使 dàshǐ
mission 使命 shǐmìng	even if 即使 jíshǐ
diplomatic mission 使团 shǐtuán	
use 使用 shǐyòng	

Ancient character

verb
noun

Compound element
亻 + 丨
people + cliff

候

Compound element
矢 *arrow*

wait; await
time; season

Note in Chinese

候 = 厂 + 矢

左边是人，右边上部是山崖，下部是箭在弦上等候发射。

🔊 **READ ALOUD**

The archers WAIT patiently by the cliff, arrows at the ready. WAIT is hòu（候）.

Stroke order

Composite capabilities: 1 2 3 4 5 6 7 8 9 10

prefix/phrase	suffix/phrase
waiting for a train(bus, etc.) 候车 hòuchē	waiting 等候 děnghòu
migrant 候鸟 hòuniǎo	when 时候 shíhòu
candidate 候选人 hòuxuǎnrén	

verb

Compound element

亻（人）*people*
亻

做

Compound element

故 = *ancient + tools/method*
故

do; make; produce; manufacture; cook; engage in; become; compose; be used as; for...

Note in Chinese

做 = 亻+ 故

远古的时候，人先要听祖先怎么说，还要看甲壳上的占卜，然后再做。所以"做"字是"人"在左，听古人之"口"在中，解读卜"文"在右，最后才做。

READ ALOUD

Before DOING anything, people used to first seek wisdom from their ancestors, then consult tortoise shells to obtain advice from the gods. DO is zuò（做）.

Stroke order

丿 亻 仁 什 仕 仕 仕 做 做 做 做

Composite capabilities: 1 2 3 4 5 6 7 8 9 10

prefix/phrase	suffix/phrase
do work 做事 zuòshì	
be a mum 做妈妈 zuò māma	
do job 做活 zuòhuó	
do business 做买卖 zuò mǎimai	
method of work 做法 zuòfǎ	

Ancient character

Compound element

 shell

noun
verb
measure word

包

bun;
bag;
package

wrap

Note in Chinese

包 = ◯ + 己

右上部分是外包的
一层，左下的部分
是能量，组合后表
示能量被一层东西
包在了里面。

Compound element

 energy/live

🍴 READ ALOUD

Chinese BUNS are delicious, but they contain a lot of calories! BUN is
bāo（包）.

Stroke order

    包

Composite capabilities: 1 2 3 4 5 6 7 8 9 10

prefix/phrase	suffix/phrase
bun 包子 bāozi	school bag 书包 shūbāo
a chartered plane 包机 bāojī	wallet 钱包 qiánbāo
forgiveness 包容 bāoróng	packing food 打包 dǎbāo
wrapper 包皮 bāopí	a sack of rice 一包米 yì bāo mǐ

Ancient character

noun

儿 *son/child*

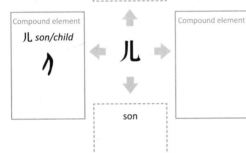

儿

Compound element

son

Note in Chinese

儿 = ノ

这是"兒"的简体。简化到把孩子的头都省略了。

READ ALOUD

This character for CHILD has two legs, but the head seems to be missing! CHILD is ér（儿）.

Stroke order

Composite capabilities: 1 2 3 4 5 6 7 8 9 10

prefix/phrase	suffix/phrase
children 儿女 érnǚ	daughter 女儿 nǚ'ér
son 儿子 érzi	children and early teenagers 少儿 shào'ér

Ancient character

Compound element

二 two elements/ number two

noun
adjective

元

element; unit; component

first; primary; basic; fundamental; principal

Compound element

 people

Note in Chinese

元 = 二 + 丿

上面代表男女二
人，下面是相交，
中国古文明认为阴
阳互动是生命之元
本与起始。

🔊 READ ALOUD

The ELEMENT of life is a result of the unity of yin and yang. ELEMENT is yuán（元）.

Stroke order

Composite capabilities: 1 2 3 4 5 6 7 8 9 10

prefix/phrase	suffix/phrase
the first year of an era 元年 yuánnián	unit 单元 dānyuán
senior statesman 元老 yuánlǎo	one dollar 一元 yìyuán
head of state 元首 yuánshǒu	
element 元素 yuánsù	

Ancient character

Compound element

屮 stop/end

adverb
noun
adjective

先

ahead; earlier;
at first; for the
time being;
before

ancestor

deceased

Compound element

儿 person

Note in Chinese

先 = 屮 + 儿

字的上部是
"止",下部是人
群。组合后表示
"人到此,再前边
就没有了",所以
是"先"。

⚙ READ ALOUD

It is the dream of every athlete to reach the finishing line AHEAD of others. AHEAD is xiān (先).

Stroke order

Composite capabilities: 1 2 3 4 5 6 7 8 9 10

prefix/phrase	suffix/phrase
before 先前 xiānqián	beforehand 事先 shìxiān
one after another 先后 xiānhòu	in advance 预先 yùxiān
Mister 先生 xiānsheng	

Ancient
character

Compound element

sky and earth

noun
verb

云

cloud

say(only for
Chinese classics)

Compound element

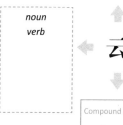 air

Note in Chinese

云 = ⟍⟍ + ♪

这是"雲"的简
体。上两横为天、
地，下为气流。天
气与地气相交，则
云雾生成。

─ 🍙 READ ALOUD ─

CLOUDS is formed by the yang energy of the sky and the yin energy of
the earth. CLOUD is yún（云）.

Stroke order

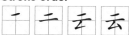

Composite capabilities: 1 2 3 4 5 6 7 8 9 10

prefix/phrase	suffix/phrase
cloud and mist 云雾 yúnwù	white clouds 白云 báiyún
the skies 云天 yúntiān	echo the views of others 人云亦云
the sport of cloud and rain 云雨	rényúnyìyún
yúnyǔ	cloudy weather 多云 duōyún

Ancient character

Compound element

 two people back to back

verb adjective

去

go; send there; remove; go in order to; in order to; be apart; away

just gone of

Compound element

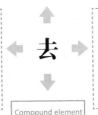 mouth

Note in Chinese

去 = 𠂇 + 凵

上边一半是夫妻两个人背对背坐着；下一半是事或物。组合后表示对事对物的态度相反，不可调和而导致离去。

READ ALOUD

When a couple argue a lot, one of them will eventually LEAVE! LEAVE is qù（去）.

Stroke order

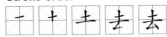

Composite capabilities: 1 2 3 4 5 6 7 8 9 10

prefix/phrase	suffix/phrase
outlet 去路 qùlù	leave 离去 líqù
last year 去年 qùnián	go on foot 走去 zǒuqù
pass away 去世 qùshì	go back 回去 huíqù
	go down 下去 xiàqù

Ancient
character

adverb

Compound element

 hand

Compound element

repetition; once
more; also;
and; again; in
addition; both
...and...

Note in Chinese

又 =

用手指计算，1为
奇数，2为偶数。
从3起，奇数又一
次出现，所以是
"又"。

🎵 **READ ALOUD**

"Three" is the first REPETITION of an odd number after the first digit.
REPETITION is yòu（又）.

Stroke order

Composite capabilities: 1 2 3 4 5 6 7 8 9 10

prefix/phrase	suffix/phrase
eating and drinking at the same time 又吃又喝 yòu chī yòu hē (He) is a teacher also is a student 又做老师又是学生 yòu zuò lǎoshī yòu shì xuésheng	again and again 一次又一次 yí cì yòu yí cì

Ancient
character

adjective
measure word

Compound element

又 *hand/bird*

Compound element

又 *hand/bird*

Note in Chinese

双 = 又 + 又

这是"雙"的简体。本来是一对雏鸟。

双

pair; dual; two;
twin; both; even;
double

🎵 READ ALOUD

This PAIR of twins are both brothers and friends to each other. PAIR is
shuāng（双）.

Stroke order

Composite capabilities: 1 2 3 4 5 6 7 8 9 10

prefix/phrase	suffix/phrase
even number 双数 shuāngshù	unrivalled 无双 wúshuāng
parents 双亲 shuāngqīn	two pairs of 两双 liǎng shuāng
both hands 双手 shuāngshǒu	
doubles(sports) 双打 shuāngdǎ	

Ancient
character

Compound element

手 arm/hand

noun
adjective

友

friend
friendly

Note in Chinese

友 = 手 + 手

这个字是两只手连
接起来组合的。

Compound element

手 arm/hand

🔊 READ ALOUD

A good FRIEND would always lend a helping hand when it is needed.
FRIEND is yǒu（友）.

Stroke order

   友

Composite capabilities: 1 2 3 4 5 6 7 8 9 10

prefix/phrase	suffix/phrase
friendly affection 友爱 yǒu'ài	friend 朋友 péngyou
friend 友人 yǒurén	kids 小朋友 xiǎopéngyǒu
friendly 友好 yǒuhǎo	fellow student 学友 xuéyǒu
	girlfriend 女朋友 nǚpéngyou

Ancient character

verb
adverb
adjective
noun
measure word
preposition

Compound element
又 *hand or again*

Compound element
寸 *measure or tool*

对

face; oppose; correct; deal with; brief; couple; with regard to

Note in Chinese

对 = 又 + 寸

这是"對"的简体。
简化后的字形更接近
古字，一边为手臂，
一边为器具，这是面
对可能出现的危险的
不可缺少的防范。

🐾 READ ALOUD

A fully armed soldier is never afraid of FACING the enemy. FACE is duì（对）.

Stroke order

フ　又　对一　对　对

Composite capabilities: 1 2 3 4 5 6 7 8 9 10

prefix/phrase	suffix/phrase
oppose 对立 duìlì	correct 很对 hěnduì
the other party 对方 duìfāng	partner 派对 pàiduì
dialogue 对话 duìhuà	a pair 一对 yí duì
with regard to; to 对 duì……	

Ancient
character

Compound element

arrows and bows

verb
noun
measure word
adjective

发

fā: *launch;
send out; utter;
rise; open up;
have a feeling;
develop; discover;
start...*

fà: *hairs*

fā: *measure word
for bullets and
shells*

Compound element

友 arm & hands

Note in Chinese

发 = ʮ + 乀

这 是 "發" 的 简
体。下面为手，上
面是进攻的机械。

🌀 READ ALOUD

Old-fashioned cannonballs have to be LAUNCHED by hand. LAUNCH is
fā（发）.

Stroke order

乚	乄	为	发	发

Composite capabilities: 1 2 3 4 5 6 7 8 9 10

prefix/phrase	suffix/phrase
shoot 发射 fāshè	set out 出发 chūfā
issue 发表 fābiǎo	a bullet 一发子弹 yì fā zǐdàn
generate power 发电 fādiàn	hairs 头发 tóufa
invent 发明 fāmíng	
developed 发达 fādá	
hairstyle 发式 fàshì	

Ancient
character

adjective
verb
noun

Compound element

 trap

难

Compound element

 bird

Note in Chinese

难 = 菓 + 隹

这是"難"的简
体。左边是一个捕
鸟的网，右边是一
只鸟。

nán: difficult;
hard

put something
into a difficult
position

nàn: disaster

🔊 READ ALOUD

It is quite DIFFICULT to catch a mistrustful bird with a net! DIFFICULT is
nán（难）.

Stroke order

Composite capabilities: 1 2 3 4 5 6 7 8 9 10

prefix/phrase	suffix/phrase
hard to do 难做 nán zuò	air disaster 空难 kōngnàn
ugly 难看 nánkàn	difficulties 困难 kùnnan
rare to get 难得 nándé	
refugee 难民 nànmín	

Ancient
character

Compound element

noun
verb

力

strength; force;
power

do all one can;
make every
effort

Compound element

Note in Chinese

力 =

这个字形表示在用
力。

🔊 **READ ALOUD**

Energy exerted through the arm produces POWER. POWER is lì（力）.

Stroke order

Composite capabilities: 1 2 3 4 5 6 7 8 9 10

prefix/phrase	suffix/phrase
strength 力气 lìqi	make strength 发力 fālì
mechanics 力学 lìxué	exert oneself 用力 yònglì
do one's best to 力求 lìqiú	do hardly 努力 nǔlì
	be a strain 吃力 chīlì

Ancient
character

Compound element

力 strength

Compound element

、（ 丫 ）
*hardship is
symbolised by a
dot.*

办

Compound element

、（ 丫 ）
*hardship is
symbolised by
another dot.*

verb

manage; do;
set up

Note in Chinese

办 = 丫 + 力 + 丫

这 是 " 辦 " 的 简
体 。 中 间 是 辛 苦
干 活 的 " 力 " (P89
力), 两 边 各 一 点 ,
表 示 事 务 或 责 任 。

READ ALOUD

It is not easy for this woman to MANAGE on her own, especially when
she has to struggle with heavy shopping! MANAGE is bàn（办）.

Stroke order

Composite capabilities: 1 2 3 4 5 6 7 8 9 10

prefix/phrase	suffix/phrase
handle affairs 办公 bàngōng	open 开办 kāibàn
deal with matter 办事 bànshì	
manage 办理 bànlǐ	

Ancient character

verb

Compound element
云 *cloud*

动

Compound element
力 *strength*

move; act;
change;
use; touch

Note in Chinese

动 = 云 + 力

这是"動"的简体。左边是"云"（P81云），右边是"力"（P89力），像一个大风扇，云被风力所推，因此才会"动"。

🎵 **READ ALOUD**

Clouds are stirred by the MOVEMENT of the air. MOVE is dòng（动）.

Stroke order

Composite capabilities: 1 2 3 4 5 6 7 8 9 10

prefix/phrase	suffix/phrase
begin construction 动工 dònggōng	sports 运动 yùndòng
interesting to listen to 动听 dòngtīng	activities 活动 huódòng
motive power 动力 dònglì	

Ancient
character

Compound element

奴 slavery

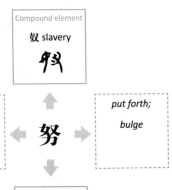

verb

努

put forth;

bulge

Compound element

力 force

Note in Chinese

努 = 奴 + 又

字的左上部是一个
人（女人），右上
部是卡住这个人的
东西，下部是一只
有"力"（P89力）
的手。组合后表明
必须加倍地劳动。

☺ READ ALOUD

Peasants working for landowners used to have to slave away in the fields
with great EFFORT. EFFORT is nǔ（努）.

Stroke order

Composite capabilities: 1 2 3 4 5 6 7 8 9 10

prefix/phrase	suffix/phrase
make great efforts 努力 nǔlì	
study hard 努力学习 nǔlì xuéxí	

Ancient
character

noun

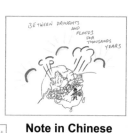

BETWEEN DROUGHTS AND FLOODS FOR THOUSANDS OF YEARS

Compound element
氵 *water*

汉

Compound element
又 *again*

the Han Dynasty

the Han nationality

Chinese language

Note in Chinese

汉 = 氵 + 莫

这是"漢"的简体。左边是水，右边是用手指表示一而再，再而三的"又"（P83又）。组合后可能是想显示中华民族具有独特的"河泛"文明史。

🔊 **READ ALOUD**

Over the centuries, the HAN people have suffered the repeated flooding of rivers. THE HAN NATIONALITY is hàn（汉）.

Stroke order

Composite capabilities: 1 2 3 4 5 6 7 8 9 10

prefix/phrase	suffix/phrase
the Han nationality 汉族 Hànzú	old man 老汉 lǎohàn
Chinese language 汉语 Hànyǔ	
Chinese character 汉字 Hànzì	

Ancient
character

noun

Compound element		Compound element
氵（水） *water* 	汁	十 *ten/a lot of* 十

juice

Note in Chinese

汁 = 氵+ 十

左边是水，右边
是单数的最大值
"十"。组合后
表示物体的"含水
量"大。

 **READ ALOUD**

This watermelon is full of JUICE! JUICE is zhī（汁）.

Stroke order

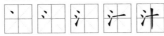

Composite capabilities: 1 2 3 4 5 6 7 8 9 10

prefix/phrase	suffix/phrase
juice 汁液 zhīyè	milk 奶汁 nǎizhī
juice 汁水 zhīshuǐ	fruit juice 果汁 guǒzhī

Ancient
character

verb
adverb

Compound element

氵（水）
waters

没

Compound element

@ + 丷

whirlpool +
hand

Note in Chinese

没 = 氵 + @ + 丷

左边是河，右边的
上头是激流，下头
是一只伸出水面的
手。表示人被激流
吞没，只剩下一只
手。

disappear; not
have; there is
not; be not so
as; less than

have not; did not

🐾 READ ALOUD

This drowning man reaching out for help is about to DISAPPEAR under
the water. DISAPPEAR is méi（没）.

Stroke order

Composite capabilities: 1 2 3 4 5 6 7 8 9 10

prefix/phrase	suffix/phrase
not have 没有 méiyǒu	appear and disappear 出没 chūmò
not have money 没钱 méi qián	submerge 淹没 yānmò
can find nothing to say 没话说	
méi huà shuō	

Ancient
character

noun

Compound element
氵（水） water

汽

Compound element
气 air/gas

steam; vapour

Note in Chinese

汽 = 氵 + 气

左边是水，右边是
气（P224气）。水
在高温下蒸发为气
体，这个"气"是
充满了水的。

READ ALOUD

STEAM is air infused with water. STEAM is qì（汽）.

Stroke order

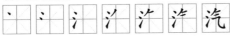

Composite capabilities: 1 **2** 3 4 5 6 7 8 9 10

prefix/phrase	suffix/phrase
automobile 汽车 qìchē	steam 水汽 shuǐqì
steamship 汽船 qìchuán	public buses 公共汽车
soda water 汽水 qìshuǐ	gōnggòng qìchē
vaporize 汽化 qìhuà	

Ancient
character

noun
verb

Compound element

⺆（水）
water/river

法

Compound element

去 go

Note in Chinese

法 = ⺆ + 去

左边是水，右边是
"去"（P82去）。
水的去向永远是向
低处，这是自然的
法则。

law; method;
way; standard;
model; magic
arts

follow; model
after

🔊 **READ ALOUD**

The LAW of nature dictates that water should always flow from high to
low. LAW is fǎ（法）.

Stroke order

丶　丶　氵　汁　汁　沣　法　法

Composite capabilities: 1 2 3 4 5 6 7 8 9 10

prefix/phrase	suffix/phrase
law 法律 fǎlǜ	civil law 民法 mínfǎ
France 法国 Fǎguó	
legal 法定 fǎdìng	
punish by law 法办 fǎbàn	

Ancient character

noun

Compound element
氵（水）river

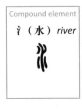

河

Compound element
可 can

river

Note in Chinese

河 = 氵 + 可

左边是水，右边是一个与人口、生活有关的肯定词"可"（P134可）。表示这个水的资源可能于人有利，即可用的水源，所以命名为"河"。

🔊 READ ALOUD

People can live most profitably by the RIVER. RIVER is hé（河）.

Stroke order

Composite capabilities: 1 2 3 4 5 6 7 8 9 10

prefix/phrase	suffix/phrase
river 河流 héliú	Yellow River 黄河 Huánghé
river waters 河水 héshuǐ	
river mouth 河口 hékǒu	
fishes of river 河鱼 héyú	

Ancient character

verb
adjective
adverb
noun

Compound element

氵（水）
waters

活

Compound element

舌（千+口）
tongue (arrow + mouth)

Note in Chinese

活 = 氵 + 舌

左边是水，右边是
舌。它的组合表示
水是一切生物得以
存活的条件。

live; save
alive; vivid;
moving

simply

works

🐳 READ ALOUD

Like all LIVING things, this whale with its tongue hanging out cannot survive without water. LIVE is huó（活）.

Stroke order

`丶 冫 氵 汁 沪 汗 汗 活 活`

Composite capabilities: 1 2 3 4 5 6 7 **8** 9 10

prefix/phrase	suffix/phrase
activities 活动 huódòng	life 生活 shēnghuó
vigour 活力 huólì	work 干活 gànhuó
workable method 活路 huólù	
running water 活水 huóshuǐ	
living 活生生 huóshēngshēng	

Ancient character

noun

Compound element
氵（水）
water/liquid

酒

Compound element
酉 *brew-jar*

Note in Chinese

酒 = 氵 + 酉

左边是掺了水的黍子，右边是容器，容器里还有发酵剂。

alcoholic drink; wine; liquor; spirits

🍷 READ ALOUD

Millet turns into WINE after fermenting in covered stone jars. WINE is jiǔ（酒）.

Stroke order

Composite capabilities: 1 2 3 4 5 6 7 8 9 10

prefix/phrase	suffix/phrase
bar 酒吧 jiǔbā	grape wine 葡萄酒 pútaojiǔ
wine cup 酒杯 jiǔbēi	beer 啤酒 píjiǔ
hotel 酒店 jiǔdiàn	

Ancient character

noun

Compound element
氵（水）water

澡

Compound element
noices +
tree / bubbles

bath; shower

Note in Chinese

澡 = 氵 + 枭

左边是雨水，右边
是一棵栖着鸟类的
大树。下起雨来，
万物都在洗浴。

⚙ **READ ALOUD**

This tree seems to be having a bubble BATH in rainwater. BATH is
zǎo（澡）.

Stroke order

| 丶 | 冫 | 氵 | 氵 | 沪 | 汧 | 汧 | 渓 | 澩 | 澡 | 澡 |

| 澡 | 澡 | 澡 | 澡 | 澡 |

Composite capabilities: 1 2 3 4 5 6 7 8 9 10

prefix/phrase	suffix/phrase
bathtub 澡盆 zǎopén public baths 澡堂 zǎotáng	take a bath 洗澡 xǐzǎo

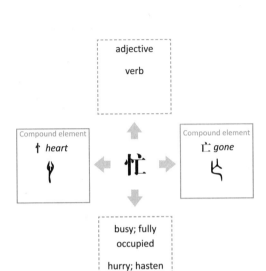

adjective

verb

Compound element
忄 *heart*

Compound element
亡 *gone*

忙

busy; fully occupied

hurry; hasten

Note in Chinese

忙 = 忄 + 亡

左边是心性，右边
是一个逃亡的人。
组合后表示心已经
不在体内。

READ ALOUD

If we are not careful, being too BUSY can lead to heart failure! BUSY is máng（忙）.

Stroke order

Composite capabilities: 1 2 3 4 5 6 7 8 9 10

prefix/phrase	suffix/phrase
be busy with 忙活 mánghuo	in a hurry 急忙 jímáng
busy person 忙人 mángrén	in a great rush 慌忙 huāngmáng

Radical 宀

Ancient
character

Compound element

宀 house

noun
adjective
verb

安

peace;
safety;
calm;
set at ease;
install

Note in Chinese

安 = 宀 + 女

上部是屋顶，下面
是一个女（P163女）
人的形象。

Compound element

女 woman

🔊 READ ALOUD

A woman good at managing a household can bring PEACE and tranquillity
into the home. PEACE is ān（安）.

Stroke order

Composite capabilities: 1 2 3 4 5 6 7 8 9 10

prefix/phrase	suffix/phrase
safety 安全 ānquán	secure 平安 píng'ān
safe and sound 安好 ānhǎo	have an easy conscience 心安理得
peace and stable 安定 āndìng	xīn'ānlǐdé

Ancient
character

Compound element
宀 house
宀

| verb | | complete; run out; end; finish |
| adverb | 完 | intact |

Compound element
二 two
二
人 person
人

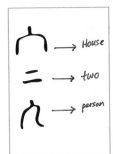

House → House
二 → two
人 → person

Note in Chinese

完 = 宀 + 二 + 人

上部是屋顶，下面的
两横代表阴与阳，
最下面是人（P63
人）。组合一起是表
示"完整"。

🔊 READ ALOUD

When two people live harmoniously under one roof, their lives become COMPLETE. COMPLETE is wán（完）.

Stroke order

Composite capabilities: 1 2 3 4 5 6 7 8 9 10

prefix/phrase	suffix/phrase
have completed 完成 wánchéng	do finish 做完 zuòwán
consummate 完美 wánměi	reading complete 看完 kànwán
finish job 完工 wángōng	endless 没完没了 méiwánméiliǎo
ended 完了 wán le	

Ancient
character

Compound element

宀 roof

adjective
verb
adverb

定

stable; fixed;
calm

decide;
subscribe

certainly;
definitely

Note in Chinese

定 = 宀 + 𤴓

上面是屋顶，下面
是一个"正"字的
结构，表示坚固而
稳定。

Compound element

正 (𤴓) stability

🎧 READ ALOUD

When a roof is securely constructed over a strong foundation, the
building is STABLE. STABLE is dìng（定）.

Stroke order

Composite capabilities: 1 2 3 4 5 6 7 8 9 10

prefix/phrase	suffix/phrase
feel at ease 定心 dìngxīn	fixed 固定 gùdìng
theorem 定理 dìnglǐ	surely 一定 yídìng
deposit 定金 dìngjīn	

Ancient character

Compound element
宀 home

adjective
noun

实

solid; practical;
true; real

reality; fruit

Note in Chinese

实 = 冖 + 头

这是"實"的简
体。上面是屋顶，
左上的两个点代表大
脑不停地运动，下边
的"大"（P123大）
是人形。

Compound element
头 head

READ ALOUD

The SOLID and efficient management of a home requires a clear head as well as good budgeting skills. SOLID is shí（实）.

Stroke order

Composite capabilities: 1 2 3 4 5 6 7 8 9 10

prefix/phrase	suffix/phrase
practical 实用 shíyòng	fact 事实 shìshí
trustworthy 实在 shízài	honest 老实 lǎoshi
experience one's skill in 实习 shíxí	
get right on the job 实干 shígàn	

Ancient
character

Compound element

宀 house

noun
adjective

客

guest; visitor;
traveller;
customer; live in
a strange place

objective

Compound element

各 each
individual

Note in Chinese

客 = 宀 + 各

上面是屋顶，中间
是彼此不相关的足
迹，下面的口表示
门径，显然是路
人，是宾客。

· 🌸 READ ALOUD ·

GUESTS arrive from all over the world to stay at this chalet-style hotel.
GUEST is kè（客）.

Stroke order

Composite capabilities: 1 2 3 4 5 6 7 8 9 10

prefix/phrase	suffix/phrase
guest 客人 kèrén	invite guest 请客 qǐngkè
polite 客气 kèqi	VIP 贵客 guìkè
guest room 客房 kèfáng	meet the customer 会客 huìkè
objective 客观 kèguān	

Ancient character

Compound element
⼧ roof
⌐

noun
pronoun
adjective
measure word

家

home; family

a specialist

my

domestic

Note in Chinese

家 = ⌐ + 豕

上部是屋顶，下部是猪：古代猪被畜养，有猪的地方便是农户的家。

Compound element
豕 pig
豕

🐷 READ ALOUD

In the old days, farmers used to keep their pigs inside the HOME. HOME is jiā（家）.

Stroke order

Composite capabilities: 1 2 3 4 5 6 7 8 9 **10**

prefix/phrase	suffix/phrase
family 家庭 jiātíng	everyone 大家 dàjiā
member of family 家人 jiārén	other people 人家 rénjia
family education 家教 jiājiào	writer 作家 zuòjiā
family letters 家书 jiāshū	a shop 一家商店 yì jiā shāngdiàn

Ancient
character

Compound element
丿丶 a bird is in
distance

| verb
conjunction | 应 | yìng: *respond;
comply with;
suit; cope with*

yīng: *should;
answer* |

Note in Chinese

应 = 广 + 鸟

这是"應"的简
体。上面是一只飞
鸟，简化后下面的
两点和一撇也是
鸟，可能是栖鸟。
这个字是暗示鸟与
鸟之间语言的对
应。

Compound element
鸟 bird

🐦 READ ALOUD

A little bird on a rooftop calls out to his three friends across the street but
they do not RESPOND. RESPOND is yìng（应）.

Stroke order

Composite capabilities: 1 2 3 4 5 6 7 8 9 10

prefix/phrase	suffix/phrase
respond 应对 yìngduì	respond 答应 dāying
accept an invitation 应邀 yìngyāo	a planted agent 内应 nèiyìng
meet an emergency 应急 yìngjí	
should to 应该 yīnggāi	

Ancient
character

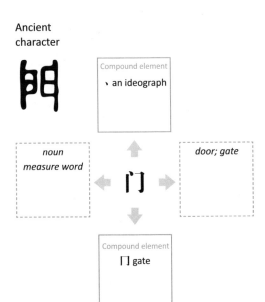

Compound element
、 an ideograph

noun
measure word

门

door; gate

Compound element
冂 gate

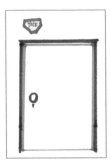

Note in Chinese

门 = 、+ 冂

这是"門"的简
体。现代城市里的
门通常没有窗子。
左上角的一点，表
示"号码"或"门
铃"。

🔊 **READ ALOUD**

This DOOR is firmly closed. DOOR is mén（门）.

Stroke order

Composite capabilities: 1 2 3 4 5 6 7 8 9 10

prefix/phrase	suffix/phrase
entrance 门口 ménkǒu	main gate 大门 dàmén
connections 门路 ménlù	front door 前门 qiánmén
admission ticket 门票 ménpiào	

Ancient
character

Compound element

门 house

verb

问

ask; inquire; exam

Note in Chinese

问 = 冂 + 口

这是"問"的简
体。门（P110门）
上开了一个口，组
合后表示问询者要
立于门外的礼节。

Compound element

口 mouth/box

🔊 READ ALOUD

It is polite to ASK at the door before dropping in on somebody. ASK is
wèn（问）.

Stroke order

Composite capabilities: 1 2 3 4 5 6 7 8 9 10

prefix/phrase	suffix/phrase
question 问题 wèntí	inquiry 提问 tíwèn
inquire 问询 wènxún	interrogate with torture
ask for direction 问路 wènlù	拷问 kǎowèn
publish 问世 wènshì	
say hello to 问候 wènhòu	

Ancient character

Compound element

门 door

noun
measure word

间

jiān:*between;*
among; room
jiàn:*space*

Note in Chinese

间 = 門 + D

这是"間"的简
体。门（P110门）
中有一个日（P205
日），表示日光从
其间透过。

Compound element

日 sun/light

READ ALOUD

Sunlight streams into the room through the window BETWEEN the curtains. BETWEEN is jiān（间）.

Stroke order

Composite capabilities: 1 2 3 4 5 6 7 8 9 10

prefix/phrase	suffix/phrase
indirect 间接 jiànjiē	spaces 空间 kōngjiān
interval 间隔 jiàngé	time 时间 shíjiān
intermittence 间歇 jiànxiē	room 房间 fángjiān

Ancient
character

noun
adverb

Compound element
辶 *walking
forward*

边

Compound element
力 *forceful
strength*

Note in Chinese

边 = 辶 + 力

这是"邊"的简体。
左下部分代表有路可
向前行进，右上是力
（P89力），力量推
着人向前行，不过
已经到了边上。

edge; side;
bound;
border

while

┌─ 🔊 READ ALOUD ────────────────────────────────

Being forced to the EDGE of a cliff can sometimes clarify the mind! EDGE
is biān（边）.

Stroke order

Composite capabilities: 1 2 3 4 5 6 7 8 9 10

prefix/phrase	suffix/phrase
border 边境 biānjìng sing while dancing 边唱边跳 biān chàng biān tiào	east side 东边 dōngbian

Ancient
character

verb
adjective

Compound element
辶 *road/walk*

Compound element
大 *large/big*

达

reach; extend;
express

eminent;
distinguished

Note in Chinese

达 = 辶 + 大

这是"達"的简
体。左下是向前行
进的路，右上是大
（P123大），表示
大步伐，这样可以
直达目的地。

🎧 READ ALOUD

Take big bold steps if you want to REACH your destination quickly! REACH
is dá（达）.

Stroke order

Composite capabilities: 1 2 3 4 5 6 7 8 9 10

prefix/phrase	suffix/phrase
achieve 达到 dádào	understand things 通达 tōngdá
take things philosophically 达观 dáguān	express 传达 chuándá
reach (agreement) 达成 dáchéng	arrive 到达 dàodá

Ancient character

verb
adverb

Compound element
辶 *walk forward*

还

Compound element
不 *no*

huán: return; go back

give or do sth.

hái: still; even more; also; passably

Note in Chinese

还 = 辶 + 不

这是"還"的简体。左下是可走的道路；右上是不（P8不）。组合后可以是多重含义：不走，就有"回还"的意思；也有想一想后"还"接着走的可能。

— 🔊 **READ ALOUD** ⸱

This traveler is a little lost—should he keep going or should he RETURN to his starting point? RETURN is huán（还）.

Stroke order

Composite capabilities: 1 2 3 4 5 6 7 8 9 10

prefix/phrase	suffix/phrase
pay one's debt 还钱 huán qián	return to home 回还 huíhuán
strike back 还手 huánshǒu	revert 归还 guīhuán
even better/no bad 还好 háihǎo	
yet/or 还是 háishì	

Ancient
character

adjective

Compound element
⻌ _walk forward_

Compound element
斤 _axe_

近

shortcut;
nearby;
access; close;
approaching;
intimate

Note in Chinese

近 = ⻌ + 斤

左下部是行走的
路，右上边是一把
斧头。很明显，是
用斧头在开辟一条
近路。

🔊 READ ALOUD

This golfer uses an axe to hack a hole in the tree so that he has a
SHORTCUT to the flag. SHORTCUT is jìn（近）.

Stroke order

Composite capabilities: 1 2 3 4 5 6 7 8 9 10

prefix/phrase	suffix/phrase
shortcut 近路 jìnlù	recently 最近 zuìjìn
short-sighted 近视 jìnshì	nearby 附近 fùjìn
in the past few days 近日 jìnrì	
modern times 近代 jìndài	

Ancient
character

verb
noun

Compound element

辶（辵）
walk forward

运

Compound element

云 *cloud*

carry; transport;
use

motion;
movement

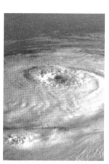

Note in Chinese

运 = 辶 + 云

这是"運"的简
体。左下部是行进
的路，右上是一团
云（P81云）。云
有了要去的路，运
而动之就是必然的
了。

READ ALOUD

Tornadoes may look like swirling clouds but they CARRY a lot more
energy! CARRY is yùn（运）.

Stroke order

Composite capabilities: 1 2 3 4 5 6 7 8 9 10

prefix/phrase	suffix/phrase
sports 运动 yùndòng	have fortune 走运 zǒuyùn
sportswear 运动衣 yùndòngyī	air transportation 空运 kōngyùn
fortune 运气 yùnqi	good luck 好运 hǎoyùn
operation 运算 yùnsuàn	Olympic Games 奥运会 Àoyùnhuì
canal 运河 yùnhé	

Ancient character

verb

Note in Chinese

退 = 辶 + 艮

左 下 部 是 行 进 的 路，右 上 边 是 与 行 进 相 对 的 "艮" 行 为，所 以 是 "退"。

Compound element
辶（走）walk

退

Compound element
艮 *changes the meaning to something related*
貝

retreat; draw back

cancel

READ ALOUD

To RETREAT is the opposite of going forwards. RETREAT is tuì（退）.

Stroke order

Composite capabilities: 1 2 3 4 5 6 7 8 9 10

prefix/phrase	suffix/phrase
refund 退还 tuìhuán	retreat 后退 hòutuì
retrogress 退步 tuìbù	
route of retreat 退路 tuìlù	
retired 退休 tuìxiū	

Ancient character

noun

measure word

Compound element
辶 *road/walk*

道

Compound element
首 *head*

Note in Chinese

道 = 辶 + 首

左下部是行走的路，右上部是首（P61 首）。头朝大道行走，就可以得"道"。老子说"大道甚夷，而民好径"，正路很平坦，但人们热衷走捷径。

way; road; doctrine

MW for a long and narrow object

- 🔊 **READ ALOUD**

Do not turn left or right when walking in the WAY of the Dao. WAY is dào（道）.

Stroke order

| 丶 | 丷 | 半 | 半 | 产 | 首 | 首 | 首 | 首 | 丶道 |

| 诮 | 道 |

Composite capabilities: 1 2 3 4 5 6 7 8 9 10

prefix/phrase	suffix/phrase
moral 道德 dàodé	a mountain pass 山间小道
road 道路 dàolù	shānjiān xiǎodào
principle 道理 dàolǐ	serve four courses
Taoist school 道家 Dàojiā	上四道菜 shàng sì dào cài

Ancient character

Compound element
土 soil

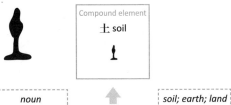

noun
adjective

土

soil; earth; land

local;
homemade;
unrefined

Compound element

Note in Chinese

土=

汉字的"土",是
指能耕耘生长的土
壤。所以这个字在
显示秧苗破土而出
的样子。

☺ READ ALOUD

Earth which can support plant growth is called SOIL. SOIL is tǔ(土).

Stroke order

Composite capabilities: 1 2 3 4 5 6 7 8 9 10

prefix/phrase	suffix/phrase
land 土地 tǔdì	one's native country 本土 běntǔ
dirt road 土路 tǔlù	territory 领土 lǐngtǔ
local dialect 土语 tǔyǔ	
Saturn 土星 Tǔxīng	

Ancient
character

Compound element

⺿ vegetation

noun
adjective
verb

草

grass

careless

draft

Note in Chinese

草 = ⺿ + 早

上边是小草的顶端,
中间是太阳,下边
是草的根茎(P206
早)。表示朝阳滋
养小草成长。

Compound element

日+十=早
sun + buds grow
=morning

🔊 READ ALOUD

GRASS looks particularly fresh in the morning sun. GRASS is cǎo(草).

Stroke order

一	十	艹	艹	甘	苩	苗	草	草

Composite capabilities: 1 2 3 4 5 6 7 8 9 10

prefix/phrase	suffix/phrase
lawn 草地 cǎodì	green grass 青草 qīngcǎo
careless 草率 cǎoshuài	make a draft 起草 qǐcǎo

Ancient
character

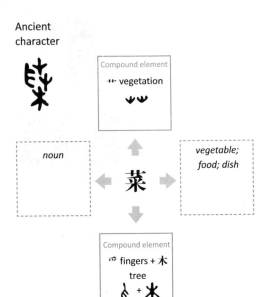

Compound element

艹 vegetation

↓↓

noun

菜

*vegetable;
food; dish*

Compound element

✍ fingers + 木
tree

☝ + 木

Note in Chinese

菜 = ↓↓ + ✍ + 木

上边是植物的叶
子，中间是手指，
意思是人工种植，下
边的木（P192木）是
植物的下部。组合
起来表示供人类食
用的蔬菜。

☝ READ ALOUD

When VEGETABLES were ready to be eaten, farmers would pick them by
hand. VEGETABLE is cài（菜）.

Stroke order

一 十 艹 艹 艹 艹 艹 苹 苹 菜

Composite capabilities: 1 2 3 **4** 5 6 7 8 9 10

prefix/phrase	suffix/phrase
cookbook 菜谱 càipǔ	green 青菜 qīngcài
menu 菜单 càidān	vegetable dish 素菜 sùcài
heart of a cabbage 菜心 càixīn	

Ancient character

Compound element
一 one

adjective
adverb

大

big; heavy; loud;
major; eldest

greatly; in a big
way

Note in Chinese

大 = 一 + 丿

字的一横，是伸展
的双臂，与其组合
的是一个"人"
（P63 人）字。

Compound element
人 person
丿

🎵 READ ALOUD

This girl is spreading her arms wide to make herself look BIG. BIG is
dà（大）.

Stroke order

Composite capabilities: 1 2 3 4 5 6 7 8 9 10

prefix/phrase	suffix/phrase
adult 大人 dàrén	open university 夜大 yèdà
grow up 大了 dà le	the number one child 老大 lǎodà
university 大学 dàxué	great 伟大 wěidà
	enlarge 放大 fàngdà

Ancient
character

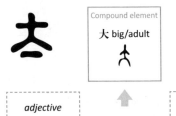

Compound element
大 big/adult

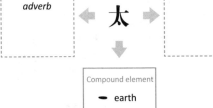

adjective
adverb

太

too; greatest

Compound element
一 earth

Note in Chinese

太 = 大 + 一

"大"（P123大）
字的中间的一点是
指示符，表示比大
更进一步。"太"
通常用来做副词，
意思是程度达到了
最大值。

🔊 READ ALOUD

If a man jumps TOO high, he risks being burnt by the sun! TOO is
tài（太）.

Stroke order

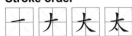

Composite capabilities: 1 2 3 4 5 6 7 8 9 10

prefix/phrase	suffix/phrase
sun 太阳 tàiyáng	wife 太太 tàitai
outer space 太空 tàikōng	
peaceful and tranquil 太平 tàipíng	
mother of an emperor 太后 tàihòu	
prince 太子 tàizǐ	
very well 太好了 tài hǎo le	
too hot 太热了 tài rè le	

Ancient
character

Compound element
大 big
人

adjective
verb
adverb

奇

strange; rare;
remarkable

be surprised

very; extremely

Compound element
可 can
人

Note in Chinese

奇 = 人 + 人

上面是大（P123大）
字形，其实是表示
双腿分开而坐；下
面是两个斜面。组
合后显出这个姿
势不平常，所以是
"奇"。

→ 💿 **READ ALOUD** →

This STRANGE man seems to be sitting astride two triangles, using a long
pole for balance. STRANGE is qí（奇）.

Stroke order

Composite capabilities: 1 2 3 4 5 6 7 8 9 10

prefix/phrase	suffix/phrase
an eccentric person 奇人 qírén	rare 稀奇 xīqí
strange 奇怪 qíguài	unusual 离奇 líqí
strange affair 奇事 qíshì	legend 传奇 chuánqí
a rare talent 奇才 qícái	

Ancient character

verb

Compound element
扌（手）hand

打

Compound element
丁 a T-Shaped object

strike; hit; break; smash; heat...

Note in Chinese

打= 手 + 个

左边是手，右边是一个T形的工具。

🔊 READ ALOUD

A hammer in hand is good for STRIKING nails into hard surfaces. STRIKE is dǎ（打）.

Stroke order

Composite capabilities: 1 2 3 4 5 6 7 8 9 10

prefix/phrase	suffix/phrase
open 打开 dǎkāi	single(sports) 单打 dāndǎ
break 打破 dǎpò	was beaten 被打 bèi dǎ
move 打动 dǎdòng	martial fighting 武打 wǔdǎ
type 打字 dǎzì	

Ancient character

verb

Compound element
扌（手）hand

扫

Compound element
彐 broom

broom; sweep;
sweep away;
eliminate;
clean up

Note in Chinese

扫 = 扌 + 彐

这是"掃"的简
体。左边是手，右
边是扫帚。

🧹 READ ALOUD

Even witches have to hold on to their BROOMS when whizzing through the air! BROOM is sǎo（扫）.

Stroke order

Composite capabilities: 1 2 3 4 5 6 7 8 9 10

prefix/phrase	suffix/phrase
sweep the floor 扫地 sǎodì	clean 打扫 dǎsǎo
eliminate illiteracy 扫盲 sǎománg	tidy and clean 清扫 qīngsǎo
feel disappointed 扫兴 sǎoxìng	
broom 扫把 sàobǎ	

Ancient character

noun	
measure word	
verb	

把

Compound element	Compound element
扌（手）*hand*	巴 *a stooped posture*

handle;
a handful of;
hold

Note in Chinese

把 = 扌 + 巴

左边是手，右边是一个弯着腰的人。

🔊 READ ALOUD

To lend a hand to someone who needs support is to provide them with a useful HANDLE. HANDLE is bǎ（把）.

Stroke order

Composite capabilities: 1 2 3 4 5 6 7 8 9 10

prefix/phrase	suffix/phrase
handle 把手 bǎshǒu	torch 火把 huǒbǎ
guard 把守 bǎshǒu	one or two 个把 gèbǎ
a handful of rice (measure word)	enforce 严把 yánbǎ
一把米 yìbǎmǐ	the handle of door 门把儿 ménbàr
pass this one to him	
把这个给他 bǎ zhège gěi tā	

Ancient character

verb
noun

Compound element
扌（手）hand

报

Compound element
⻖ obey / submit

report; repay

newspaper

Note in Chinese

报 = 幸 + ⻖

这是"報"的简体。左边是手，右边是一个以躬身来表示服从的人。

🎵 **READ ALOUD**

When an official REPORTS to her superior, it is customary for her to bow her head in obeisance. REPORT is bào（报）.

Stroke order

Composite capabilities: 1 2 3 4 5 6 7 8 9 10

prefix/phrase	suffix/phrase
repay 报答 bàodá	reciprocate 回报 huíbào
report 报告 bàogào	poster 海报 hǎibào
sign up 报名 bàomíng	
newspapers 报纸 bàozhǐ	

Ancient
character

Compound element
小 small

adjective
adverb
noun

小

little; small;
young

of short duration

children

Compound element

Note in Chinese

小 = 小

三个短小的笔画,
表示微小。形状很
像一个幼儿,刚刚
可以站起来,保持
平衡。

🔊 READ ALOUD

This character looks like a LITTLE penguin trying to balance itself with its
two wings. LITTLE is xiǎo(小).

Stroke order

Composite capabilities: 1 2 3 4 5 6 7 8 9 10

prefix/phrase	suffix/phrase
child 小孩儿 xiǎoháir	size 大小 dàxiǎo
primary school 小学 xiǎoxué	immature 幼小 yòuxiǎo
drizzle 小雨 xiǎoyǔ	
snacks 小吃 xiǎochī	
in one's childhood 小时候 xiǎoshíhou	

Ancient
character

Compound element
 few

adjective

verb

adverb

noun

 少

shǎo: *few; little; less*

be short; lose; stop

a little while

shào: *young early youth*

Note in Chinese

少=

只有四个小点，表示少量。

Compound element

🎵 READ ALOUD

There seems to be too FEW beans to go round the table! FEW is shǎo（少）.

Stroke order

Composite capabilities: 1 2 3 4 5 6 7 8 9 10

prefix/phrase	suffix/phrase
minority 少数 shǎoshù minority nationality 少数民族 shǎoshù mínzú rare 少有 shǎoyǒu infrequent 少见 shǎojiàn teenage 少年 shàonián young girl 少女 shàonǚ	how many 多少 duōshao teen-agers 青少年 qīngshàonián

Ancient character

Compound element

口 mouth

noun
measure word
verb

号

howl; bugle; horn

number; date;
name; mark

Note in Chinese

号 = 口 + 丂

这是"號"的简体。上面是大"口"，下面是器具在鼓动。表示发出很大的声音。

Compound element

丂 tool/horn

🔊 READ ALOUD

The winds tend to HOWL bitterly in the Yorkshire moors. HOWL is hào（号）.

Stroke order

丨	冂	口	号	号

Composite capabilities: 1 2 3 4 5 6 7 8 9 10

prefix/phrase	suffix/phrase
bugle 号角 hàojiǎo	4th March 三月四号
verbal command 号令 hàolìng	Sānyuè Sìhào
number 号码 hàomǎ	title 称号 chēnghào

Ancient character

verb
preposition

Compound element

口 *mouth*

叫

Compound element

彐 *stretch*

yell; shout; cry;
call; order; ask;
name; allow

Note in Chinese

叫 = 口 + 彐

左边是张大的口，
右边是展开的身
体，组合后表示大
声地喊叫。

🔊 READ ALOUD

Teachers love to use loudspeakers when YELLING at children in the schoolyard. YELL is jiào（叫）.

Stroke order

丨	𠮛	口	叫	叫

Composite capabilities: 1 2 3 4 5 6 7 8 9 10

prefix/phrase	suffix/phrase
shout 叫喊 jiàohǎn	name is 名叫 míngjiào
hawk 叫卖 jiàomài	shout loudly 大叫 dàjiào
be called 叫作 jiàozuò	

Ancient character

Compound element

circle/encircle

verb

conjunction

adverb

可

be able to; approve; may; good to; can; fit

but

Note in Chinese

可 = 丁 + 口

这个字的原意是张口唱歌所发出的声音，后用作副词和转折连词等。

Compound element

口 mouth/ taste

🔊 **READ ALOUD**

You won't BE ABLE TO taste this delicious piece of chocolate unless you open your mouth! BE ABLE TO is kě（可）.

Stroke order

Composite capabilities: 1 2 3 4 5 6 7 8 9 **10**

prefix/phrase	suffix/phrase
lovely 可爱 kě'ài	not allow 不可 bùkě
good to taste 可口 kěkǒu	approve 认可 rènkě
annoying 可气 kěqì	not necessary 大可不必 dàkěbúbì
possible 可能 kěnéng	
but 可是 kěshì	

Ancient
character

Compound element

middle/balance

noun

史

history

Note in Chinese

史 = 屮 + 乀

这个字由"中"与
"手臂"组合而成。
"中"（P17中）是
表示"公正"，手
是表示一个史官正
在书写历史。

Compound element

hand/tool

🎤 **READ ALOUD**

When writing HISTORY, it is important to maintain a balanced and
detached viewpoint. HISTORY is shǐ（史）。

Stroke order

Composite capabilities: 1 2 3 4 5 6 7 8 9 10

prefix/phrase	suffix/phrase
history book 史书 shǐshū	history 历史 lìshǐ
historical facts 史实 shǐshí	world history 世界史 shìjièshǐ
prehistoric 史前 shǐqián	
official historian 史官 shǐguān	

Ancient character

verb

Compound element
口 *mouth*

吃

Compound element
乞 *beg*

eat

Note in Chinese

吃 = 口 + 乞

左边是口，右边是
一个人跪着乞求的
姿势。

🔊 **READ ALOUD**

This boy is begging for something to EAT. EAT is chī（吃）.

Stroke order

| 丨 | 口 | 口 | 口 | 口 | 吃 |

Composite capabilities: 1 2 3 4 5 6 7 8 9 10

prefix/phrase	suffix/phrase
the culture of eating 吃文化 Chīwénhuà	snacks 小吃 xiǎochī
the table manner 吃相 chīxiàng	stutter 口吃 kǒuchī
be very popular 吃香 chīxiāng	have knowledge of eating 会吃 huìchī

Ancient character

Compound element

 mum

noun

后

behind; after; last; offspring; empress; queen

Compound element

 child

Note in Chinese

后 =  + 

上面是一个女（P163女）人，下面是一个张开的口，是妇女生子有“后代”的意思；而走得迟缓，落于人“后”则是一个方位词。

READ ALOUD

Children like to follow closely BEHIND their mothers. BEHIND is hòu（后）.

Stroke order

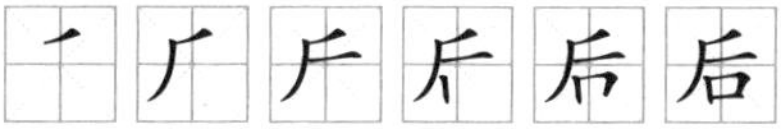

Composite capabilities: 1 2 3 4 5 6 7 8 9 10

prefix/phrase	suffix/phrase
next generation 后代 hòudài	queen 王后 wánghòu
at the back 后面 hòumiàn	at the last 最后 zuìhòu
consequence 后果 hòuguǒ	after 以后 yǐhòu
draw back 后退 hòutuì	
the day after tomorrow 后天 hòutiān	

Ancient
character

Compound element
夕 moon/night

noun
verb
adjective
measure word

名

name; fame;
excuse

given name;
express

famous

Compound element
口 mouth

Note in Chinese

名 = 𝐃 + 𝐔

上边是月夜，下边
是张大的口：黑夜
看不清对方，所以
呼名相识。

🌀 READ ALOUD

On a dark evening, people have to call out each other's NAMES in order
to locate them. NAME is míng（名）.

Stroke order

Composite capabilities: 1 2 3 4 5 6 7 8 9 10

prefix/phrase	suffix/phrase
name 名字 míngzi	full name 姓名 xìngmíng
famous person 名人 míngrén	be famous 有名 yǒumíng
noun 名词 míngcí	
famous wine 名酒 míngjiǔ	
nominal 名义 míngyì	

Ancient
character

Compound element

牛 cow

verb

告

tell;
accuse ;
ask for;
declare

Note in Chinese

告 = + ∪

上部是"牛"（P221
牛 ）字 ， 下 面 是
"口"：牛为古代
祭祖之物，以祷告
祖先。

Compound element

口 mouth

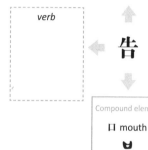

🔊 **READ ALOUD**

Cows cannot speak, so it is difficult for them to INFORM us of their
feelings. INFORM is gào（告）.

Stroke order

      告

Composite capabilities: 1 2 3 4 5 6 7 8 9 10

prefix/phrase	suffix/phrase
tell 告诉 gàosu	prosecutor 原告 yuángào
say good-bye 告别 gàobié	defendant 被告 bèigào
ask for leave 告退 gàotuì	
inform against 告发 gàofā	

Ancient character

verb

Compound element

口 *speak/mouth*

听

Compound element

斤 *axe*

listen;
hear; heed;
administer; allow

Note in Chinese

听 = 口 + 斤

左边是"口",右边是"斤"——斧头。孔子说的"非礼勿听",我们可以解释为耳朵里有一把斧头,坏话就砍去不要听。人应该明辨是非,不要听信蜚语。

🌐 READ ALOUD

In the presence of malicious speech, Confucius advises us not to LISTEN, but to cut off our ears with a metaphorical axe. LISTEN is tīng(听).

Stroke order

Composite capabilities: 1 2 3 4 5 6 7 8 9 10

prefix/phrase	suffix/phrase
wait for 听候 tīnghòu	reading and listening 视听 shìtīng
heard 听说 tīngshuō	monitor 监听 jiāntīng
hearing/listening 听力 tīnglì	
obey 听话 tīnghuà	

Ancient character

noun
adjective
verb
preposition
conjunction

Compound element		Compound element
禾 *crops*	和	口 *mouth*

Note in Chinese
和 = 禾 + 口
左边是禾穗，右边
是"口"。中国讲
究"吃的文化"，
有饭吃，天下就和
平。

harmony; peace

kind

draw

together with

and

🌀 READ ALOUD

When the harvest is good, mouths can be fed and HARMONY ensues in the community. HARMONY is hé（和）.

Stroke order

Composite capabilities: 1 2 3 4 5 6 7 8 9 10

prefix/phrase	suffix/phrase
peace 和平 hépíng	mild 温和 wēnhé
become reconciled 和解 héjiě	republic 共和 gònghé
harmonious 和谐 héxié	you and I 你和我 nǐ hé wǒ
gentle 和气 héqì	

Ancient
character

Note in Chinese

唱 = 口 + 昌

左边是"口"，右边是一个人站在一尊金属的容器里击奏。表示边演奏边开口而歌。

```
       ┌─────────────┐
       │    verb      │
       └─────────────┘
              ↑
┌──────────────┐   ┌──────────────┐
│Compound element│  │Compound element│
│  口 mouth    │ ← 唱 → │ 昌 flourishing│
│   凵         │   │   昌         │
└──────────────┘   └──────────────┘
              ↓
       ┌─────────────┐
       │    sing      │
       └─────────────┘
```

🎵 **READ ALOUD**

Three voices SINGING together is called a trio. SING is chàng（唱）.

Stroke order

| 丨 | 冂 | 口 | 叮 | 叮 | 唱 | 唱 | 唱 | 唱 | 唱 | 唱 |

Composite capabilities: 1 2 3 4 5 6 7 8 9 10

prefix/phrase	suffix/phrase
sing song 唱歌 chànggē	chorus 合唱 héchàng
lyrics 唱词 chàngcí	
record player 唱机 chàngjī	
the way of singing 唱法 chàngfǎ	

Ancient character

verb

Compound element

口 *mouth*

喝

Compound element

曷 *physical stretch*

drink

Note in Chinese

喝 = 口 + 曷

左边是"口",右边的字形是竭尽全力的样子,是发出口令,喝止别人;后又义为"饮"。

READ ALOUD

DRINKING too much water can stretch our stomachs! DRINK is hē(喝).

Stroke order

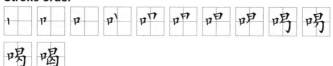

Composite capabilities: 1 2 3 4 5 6 7 8 9 10

prefix/phrase	suffix/phrase
drink tea 喝茶 hē chá drink wine 喝酒 hē jiǔ	eating and drinking 吃喝 chīhē

Ancient character

Compound element

四 four

numeral

four

Note in Chinese

四 =

这个字古体字是在
一、二、三的基础
上发展的。但是后
来把它横过来，上
下又各加了一横。

Compound element

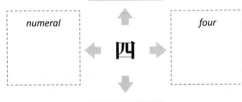

☉ READ ALOUD

This is a gated community with a single lane through the centre. The speed limit is only FOUR miles per hour. FOUR is sì（四）.

Stroke order

Composite capabilities: 1 2 3 4 5 6 7 8 9 10

prefix/phrase	suffix/phrase
the four directions 四方 sìfāng	fourteen 十四 shísì
forty 四十 sìshí	
four seasons 四季 sìjì	
extended in all directions 四通八达 sìtōngbādá	

Ancient character

verb
measure word

Compound element
口
four-side-wall

Compound element
口
mouth

回

return; turn to; answer to; report back; decline

chapter; time

Note in Chinese

回 = 口 + 口

两个口，大口套小口。原意可能是水流的回旋，后来引申为返回。

☺ READ ALOUD

To go home is to RETURN to one's roots. RETURN is huí（回）.

Stroke order

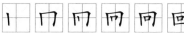

Composite capabilities: 1 2 3 4 5 6 7 8 9 10

prefix/phrase	suffix/phrase
return home 回家 huí jiā	return trip 来回 láihuí
repay 回报 huíbào	refund 找回 zhǎohuí
wire back 回电 huídiàn	three times 三回 sān huí
return to one's country 回国 huí guó	

Ancient character

noun
verb
adjective
measure word

Compound element

O *circular*

团

Compound element

才 *talent/ specialist*

Note in Chinese

团 = O +

这是"團"的简
体。简化后的中间
是"才",意思是
有特别的能力;外
面的四围是拥戴的
意思。组合后表达
人们以中间者为核
心的团结与整体的
精神。

group; regiment; ball

roll something into a ball; unite

round; circular

🔊 **READ ALOUD**

The potential power of a GROUP lies in their common cause and peaceful collaboration. GROUP is tuán（团）.

Stroke order

Composite capabilities: 1 2 3 4 5 6 7 8 9 10

prefix/phrase	suffix/phrase
unite 团结 tuánjié	group 集团 jítuán
reunion 团圆 tuányuán	delegation group 代表团
group 团体 tuántǐ	dàibiǎotuán
regimental commander 团长 tuánzhǎng	

Ancient
character

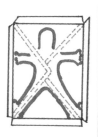

noun
verb
conjunction

Compound element

口 *box*

O

因

Compound element

大 *adult*

reason; cause;
follow; carry on

because of

because

Note in Chinese

因 = O +

这个字可能是古代
一种供人坐息的
编织物，中间的
"大"（P123大）
是图案，四方的外
围是整体。后来引
申为原"因"。

🎧 READ ALOUD

There must be a good REASON why this man is standing inside a box.
REASON is yīn（因）。

Stroke order

Composite capabilities: 1 2 **3** 4 5 6 7 8 9 10

prefix/phrase	suffix/phrase
because 因为 yīnwèi	reason 原因 yuányīn
therefore 因此 yīncǐ	cause of formation 成因 chéngyīn
thus 因而 yīn'ér	
cause and effect 因果 yīnguǒ	

Ancient character

Compound element

口 wall

noun

国

country; state; nation

Compound element

玉 jade/ treasure

王

Note in Chinese

国 = ⃝ + 王

这是"國"的简体。中间是王的印章，四围是城堡。组合后表示王与四面的城墙所围起来的地方是国家。

READ ALOUD

City walls guard the emperor's jade seal, symbol of the COUNTRY's power and dignity. COUNTRY is guó（国）.

Stroke order

Composite capabilities: 1 2 3 4 5 6 7 8 9 10

prefix/phrase	suffix/phrase
state 国家 guójiā	China 中国 Zhōngguó
member of nation 国民 guómín	United Kingdom 英国 Yīngguó
territory 国土 guótǔ	U.S.A. 美国 Měiguó
parliament 国会 guóhuì	U.N. 联合国 Liánhéguó
king 国王 guówáng	

Ancient
character

Compound element

山 mountain

Note in Chinese

山 =

三个山峰连在一起
是汉字"山"。

noun

mountain; hill

山

Compound element

🔊 READ ALOUD

This character looks just like a range of MOUNTAINS. MOUNTAIN is
shān（山）.

Stroke order

Composite capabilities: 1 2 3 4 5 6 7 8 9 10

prefix/phrase	suffix/phrase
hilltop 山头 shāntóu	big mountain 大山 dàshān
mountain pass 山路 shānlù	high hill 高山 gāoshān
landscape 山水 shānshuǐ	
goat 山羊 shānyáng	

Ancient character

adverb

quite very

Note in Chinese

很 = 彳 + 艮

左边是人在街市的
行止，右边是一个
不情愿的形象，表
示行走不顺利，或
行为不服从。后来
转义，做副词，表
示程度。

Compound element
彳 in the street

很

Compound element
艮 changes
the meaning
to something
related

very; very much;
quite

🔊 **READ ALOUD**

Crossing the street in heavy traffic can be VERY difficult, especially in Beijing! VERY is hěn（很）.

Stroke order

| ノ | ク | 彳 | 彳フ | 彳コ | 彳ヨ | 很 | 很 | 很 |

Composite capabilities: 1 2 3 4 5 6 7 8 9 10

prefix/phrase	suffix/phrase
very good 很好 hěn hǎo	very good indeed 好得很 hǎodehěn
very tall 很高 hěn gāo	
fair enough 很公平 hěn gōngpíng	

Ancient
character

verb
adjective
auxiliary word

Compound element

彳 road/action

得

Compound element

贝+手

treasure + hands

obtain; get; gain;
result in

used after a verb
or an adjective

need; have to

Note in Chinese

得 = 彳 + 貝 + 手
左边是街，右边的
上面是财富，下面
是手。组合的意思
是沿着道走，人
（手）会获得财
富。

☞ READ ALOUD

Follow this road and you will OBTAIN a treasure—a little shell that can fit
into the palm of your hand. OBTAIN is dé（得）.

Stroke order

| ノ | ク | 彳 | 彳 | 彴 | 彴 | 徂 | 徂 | 徂 | 得 | 得 |

Composite capabilities: 1 2 3 4 5 6 7 8 9 10

prefix/phrase	suffix/phrase
get 得到 dédào	complacent 自得 zìdé
fall ill 得病 débìng	very well 好得很 hǎodehěn
need go 得去 děi qù	

Ancient
character

noun

Compound element
彳 *street*
彳

街

Compound element
圭+亍
soil-bricks+street
圭 + 亍

Note in Chinese

街 = 彳 + 圭 + 亍

左边是街道，右边
也是街道，中间是
建筑物。组合后是
街市的意思。

street; road;
market

🎧 READ ALOUD

The cobbled area between houses where people walk is a STREET. STREET
is jiē（街）.

Stroke order

 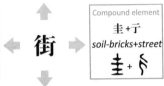

Composite capabilities: 1 2 3 4 5 6 7 8 9 10

prefix/phrase	suffix/phrase
street 街道 jiēdào	main street 大街 dàjiē
name of street 街名 jiēmíng	ancient street 古街 gǔjiē
street lamb 街灯 jiēdēng	street market 街市 jiēshì
street corner 街头 jiētóu	

Ancient character

noun
verb

Compound element
开 open

形

Compound element
彡 light/shadow

shape; form; body

appear; contrast

Note in Chinese

形 = 开 + 彡

左边是被打开（P9 开）的窗子，右边是阳光照射进来。组合后，表明光与形的关系。

🔊 READ ALOUD

Light coming through latticed windows throws beautiful SHAPES on the wall. SHAPE is xíng（形）.

Stroke order

Composite capabilities: 1 2 3 4 5 6 7 8 9 10

prefix/phrase	suffix/phrase
image 形象 xíngxiàng	appearance 外形 wàixíng
describe 形容 xíngróng	shape of body 体形 tǐxíng
form 形式 xíngshì	square-shaped 方形 fāngxíng
be always together 形影不离	
xíngyǐngbùlí	

Ancient
character

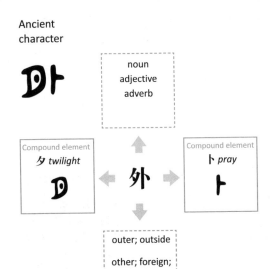

noun
adjective
adverb

Compound element
夕 *twilight*

Compound element
卜 *pray*

外

outer; outside

other; foreign;
unofficial

besides

Note in Chinese

外 = ꭰ + 卜
左边是夕阳已落，
右边是一个人在昏
暗下祈祷。

🔊 READ ALOUD

In rural communities, evening prayers often took place OUTSIDE amidst
nature. OUTSIDE is wài（外）.

Stroke order

Composite capabilities: 1 2 3 4 5 6 7 8 9 10

prefix/phrase	suffix/phrase
outside 外边 wàibian	foreign country 国外 guówài
foreign countries 外国 wàiguó	internal and external 内外 nèiwài
foreigner 外宾 wàibīn	overseas 海外 hǎiwài
foreign language 外语 wàiyǔ	
coat 外衣 wàiyī	

Ancient
character

adjective
verb
noun
auxiliary word
adverb

Compound element
夕 twilight

多

Compound element
夕 twilight

Note in Chinese

多 = 夕 + 夕

字的上下各一个夕
晖，太多了。

many
have more
over a specified
amount
how

✎ READ ALOUD

One twilight is beautiful, but two would be one too many MANY.MANY is
duō（多）.

Stroke order

Composite capabilities: 1 2 3 4 5 6 7 8 9 **10**

prefix/phrase	suffix/phrase
meddlesome 多事 duōshì	
have more 多出 duōchū	
majority 多数 duōshù	
how high is 多高 duō gāo	

Ancient character

Compound element

 house and dancers

| noun verb | | *dance* *dance with sth; flourish* |

舞

Compound element

舛 disorder/feet

Note in Chinese

舞 = 𣥺 + 舛

上面是人们提着丰收的谷穗，下面是昏暗中人们纷乱的脚步。组合后显示人们载歌载舞。

📢 READ ALOUD

This chorus line is DANCING with linked arms and nimble feet. DANCE is wǔ（舞）.

Stroke order

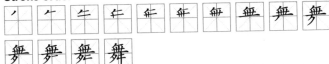

Composite capabilities: 1 2 3 4 5 6 7 8 9 10

prefix/phrase	suffix/phrase
dance 舞蹈 wǔdǎo	dance 跳舞 tiàowǔ
dancing partner 舞伴 wǔbàn	ballet 芭蕾舞 bālěiwǔ
dancing party 舞会 wǔhuì	modern dance 现代舞 xiàndàiwǔ

Ancient character

Compound element

自 head

noun

夏

summer

Compound element

ヒ∃ + ㄗ

hands + feet

Note in Chinese

夏 = 自 + ヒ∃ + ㄗ

上部是戴着帽子的
头（P2头），下面
是甩开的两臂和匆
匆行走的脚步。

🎵 READ ALOUD

People who deliver ice in the height of SUMMER have two requirements:
a big hat and an ability to walk fast! SUMMER is xià（夏）.

Stroke order

Composite capabilities: 1 **2** 3 4 5 6 7 8 9 10

prefix/phrase	suffix/phrase
summer 夏天 xiàtiān	early summer 初夏 chūxià
the lunar calendar 夏历 xiàlì	the height of summer 盛夏 shèngxià
the end of summer season	
夏末 xiàmò	

Ancient
character

noun

Compound element

饣（食）
food or eat

饭

Compound element

反 *hand with
tools or opposite*

Note in Chinese

饭 = 食 + 反

这是"饭"的简体。
左边是食（P300食）
物，右边是一只手
执着进食的器具。

cooked rice;
meal

🍴 READ ALOUD

Westerners eat with knives and forks, but the Chinese serve their RICE
with chopsticks. RICE is fàn（饭）.

Stroke order

Composite capabilities: 1 2 3 4 5 6 7 8 9 10

prefix/phrase	suffix/phrase
meal 饭菜 fàncài	cooked rice 米饭 mǐfàn
hotel 饭店 fàndiàn	
dining hall 饭厅 fàntīng	

Ancient character

adjective
adverb
verb

Compound element

彳（食）
food/eat

饱

Compound element

包 *wrap*

Note in Chinese

饱 = +

这是"飽"的简体。
左边是食（P300食）
物，右边是包（P77
包）。组合后表示
被食物所充满。

be full;
plump; fully;
satisfy

✿ READ ALOUD

Buns are not easy to digest. They often make your stomach feel round and FULL. BE FULL is bǎo（饱）.

Stroke order

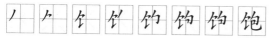

Composite capabilities: 1 2 3 4 5 6 7 8 9 10

prefix/phrase	suffix/phrase
plump 饱满 bǎomǎn	eat one's full 吃饱 chībǎo
experience fully 饱尝 bǎocháng	have a good meal
saturation 饱和 bǎohé	大饱口福 dàbǎokǒufú

Ancient
character

adjective
verb
noun

Compound element
饣（食）
food/eat

饿

Compound element
我 *I/me*

Note in Chinese

饿 = 食 + 我

这是"餓"的简体。
左边是食（P300食）
物，右边是"我"
（P201我）字。

hungry
hunger
starve

- 🌀 **READ ALOUD**

    When I am HUNGRY I need to eat straightaway! HUNGRY is è（饿）.

Stroke order

| ノ | ⺊ | 饣 | 𣥂 | 𣥂 | 饣 | 铲 | 饫 | 饿 | 饿 |

Composite capabilities: **1** 2 3 4 5 6 7 8 9 10

prefix/phrase	suffix/phrase
be hungry 饿了 è le miss a meal 饿一顿 è yí dùn	starve 饥饿 jī'è

Ancient
character

unborn to
born

pronoun

己

*oneself;
personal;
one's own*

Compound element

Compound element

Note in Chinese

己 = 己 (己)

这个字表示胎儿出
生以后由原来在母
亲体内的头朝下变
为了头朝上，意思
是已经有了生命，
有了"自己"。

🔊 READ ALOUD

A baby's head turns upwards once he is born. He has acquired an
individual existence and a sense of SELF. SELF is jǐ (己).

Stroke order

Composite capabilities: 1 2 3 4 5 6 7 8 9 10

prefix/phrase	suffix/phrase
one's own side 己方 jǐfāng	oneself 自己 zìjǐ
one's duty 己任 jǐrèn	selfish 利己 lìjǐ

Ancient character

verb
noun
measure word

Compound element
弓 *bowstring*

张

Compound element
长 *long/grow*

Note in Chinese

张 = 弓 + 长

这是"張"的简体。
左边是弓上的丝弦，
右边是"长"（P21
长），可以看成是
一个人把箭搭在弓
上。

spread; open;
stretch; set out;
magnify; look

a popular
surname

🔊 READ ALOUD

Arrows fly from the bow in all directions, like a peacock SPREADING its
tail. SPREAD is zhāng（张）.

Stroke order

Composite capabilities: 1 2 **3** 4 5 6 7 8 9 10

prefix/phrase	suffix/phrase
open the bow 张弓 zhānggōng	open a business 开张 kāizhāng
open up 张开 zhāngkāi	a table 一张桌子 yì zhāng zhuōzi
ask for a favour 张口 zhāngkǒu	
Mr. Zhang 张先生 Zhāng xiānsheng	

Ancient
character

Compound element

女 woman

noun

女

woman;
female;
daughter; girl

Note in Chinese

女 =

古代女人做事，常
常需要屈着膝。

Compound element

🎧 **READ ALOUD**

This character looks like a WOMAN sitting crossed-legged in a yoga pose!
WOMAN is nǚ（女）.

Stroke order

Composite capabilities: 1 2 3 4 5 6 7 8 9 10

prefix/phrase	suffix/phrase
woman 女人 nǚrén	women 妇女 fùnǚ
female 女子 nǚzǐ	sons and daughters 儿女 érnǚ
daughter 女儿 nǚ'ér	wife and daughter 妻女 qīnǚ
the Queen 女王 nǚwáng	
hostess 女主人 nǚzhǔrén	

Ancient
character

noun
verb
adjective

Compound element
女 woman

奶

Compound element
乃 breast

milk; breasts

suckle; feed;
breast

Note in Chinese

奶 = 女 + 乃

左边是女性（P163
女），右边是乳房
的轮廓。

🔊 READ ALOUD

The radical on the right of this character describes the shape of a
woman's breasts, where MILK is produced to nourish her children. MILK
is nǎi（奶）.

Stroke order

Composite capabilities: 1 2 3 4 5 6 7 8 9 10

prefix/phrase	suffix/phrase
milk 奶汁 nǎizhī	cow milk 牛奶 niúnǎi
cow 奶牛 nǎiniú	sheep milk 羊奶 yángnǎi
grandmother 奶奶 nǎinai	feeding 喂奶 wèinǎi
tea with milk 奶茶 nǎichá	

Ancient character

adjective
adverb
verb

Compound element
女 *woman*

好

Compound element
子 *child*

Note in Chinese

好 = 女 + 子

左边是女（P163
女）性，右边是幼
子（P169子）。

hǎo: good; fine;
be in good health

be good to; the
better to

hào: like; love; be
liable to

🞂 READ ALOUD

Mother and child usually have a GOOD relationship. GOOD is hǎo（好）.

Stroke order

Composite capabilities: 1 2 3 4 5 6 7 8 9 10

prefix/phrase	suffix/phrase
good person 好人 hǎorén	friendly 友好 yǒuhǎo
good matter 好事 hǎoshì	hobby 爱好 àihào
nice weather 好天 hǎotiān	
good looking 好看 hǎokàn	
curiosity 好奇 hàoqí	

Ancient
character

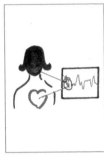

| verb |
| conjunction |

Compound element		Compound element
女 *woman*	如	口 *mouth*

similar; be like;
as; as if; be as sth
as; such as; for
instance

if; in case(of); in
the event of

Note in Chinese

如 = 女 + 口

左边是女（P163女）
性，右边是口。组
合后一种解释是"女
人心口如一"。

🎯 READ ALOUD

Women have no trouble speaking from the heart. Their words and
feelings are often very SIMILAR. SIMILAR is rú（如）.

Stroke order

Composite capabilities: 1 2 3 4 5 6 7 8 9 10

prefix/phrase	suffix/phrase
is like 如同 rútóng	for example 比如 bǐrú
reflect the things as they really are	not as good as 不如 bùrú
如实 rúshí	such as 例如 lìrú
like a stranded fish returns into water	
如鱼得水 rúyúdéshuǐ	
if 如果 rúguǒ	

Ancient character

Compound element

ᔔ working tool

noun

妻

wife

Compound element

女 woman

仈

Note in Chinese

妻 = ᔔ + 仈

上边是手，拿着一个扫把，下边是女（P163女）性。组合后表达了一种"女人做妻子后要承担家务"的看法。

🔊 READ ALOUD

Within the family, it was often the WIFE who did all the baking. WIFE is qī（妻）.

Stroke order

Composite capabilities: 1 2 3 4 5 6 7 8 9 10

prefix/phrase	suffix/phrase
wife 妻子 qīzi	good wife 贤妻 xiánqī
wife and daughter 妻女 qīnǚ	ex-wife 前妻 qiánqī
wife and children 妻儿 qī'ér	
wife and children 妻小 qīxiǎo	
breaking up of one's family 妻离子散 qīlízǐsàn	

Ancient character

noun
verb

Compound element
女 woman

姓

Compound element
生 give birth / produce

surname

be called

Note in Chinese

姓 = 女 + 生

这个字由女（P163女）在左，生（P22生）在右组成。中国的远古，通常孩子只认识母亲，所以母亲是姓氏的来源。

- 🎧 READ ALOUD -

Children used to be given their mother's SURNAME because she was often the only parent they knew. SURNAME is xìng（姓）.

Stroke order

Composite capabilities: 1 2 3 4 5 6 7 8 9 10

prefix/phrase	suffix/phrase
full name 姓名 xìngmíng surname 姓氏 xìngshì	surname(for a question) 贵姓 guìxìng

Ancient character

Compound element

子 child/son

noun		son; child;
pronoun	子	person; seed
adjective		you
		young

Compound element

Note in Chinese

子 = 𝔜

一个戴着帽子的孩子，张开手臂，蹒跚学步。

🌀 READ ALOUD

This character looks like a CHILD learning to walk, trying to balance himself with outstretched arms. CHILD is zǐ（子）.

Stroke order

Composite capabilities: 1 2 3 4 5 6 7 8 9 10

prefix/phrase	suffix/phrase
subsidiary company 子公司 zǐgōngsī	son 儿子 érzi
children and grandchildren 子孙 zǐsūn	grandson 孙子 sūnzi
sons and daughters 子女 zǐnǚ	kids 孩子 háizi
meridian line 子午线 zǐwǔxiàn	house 房子 fángzi
	Confucius 孔子 Kǒngzǐ

Ancient character

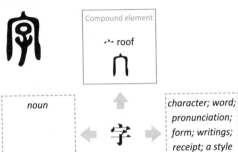

Compound element

宀 roof

noun

字

character; word;
pronunciation;
form; writings;
receipt; a style

Compound element

子 child

Note in Chinese

字 = 宀 + 子

上面是屋顶，下面
是孩子（P169子）。
组合后表达孩子的
生活要以读书写字
为主。

✏ READ ALOUD

This child is writing down the CHARACTERS he had learnt at school.
CHARACTER is zì（字）.

Stroke order

Composite capabilities: 1 2 3 **4** 5 6 7 8 9 10

prefix/phrase	suffix/phrase
dictionary 字典 zìdiǎn	Chinese character 汉字 Hànzì
font size 字号 zìhào	calligraphy 毛笔字 máobǐzì
letter 字母 zìmǔ	ancient character 古字 gǔzì
form of a written character 字体 zìtǐ	

Ancient
character

Compound element

扌+ X =
hands+
knowledge

verb
noun

学

study; imitate

learning;
knowledge

Compound element

∩ + 孑

roof + child

Note in Chinese

学 = ⺍ + ∩ + 孑

这是"學"的简体。
简化后上面的三画可
能表示动手、知识和
技能，中间是屋子，
下面是孩子（P169
子）。组合后意思
为学习。

🔊 **READ ALOUD**

A child who STUDIES diligently will one day grasp the three-pronged
knowledge of courage, wisdom and compassion. STUDY is xué（学）.

Stroke order

`	⺍	⺍	⺍	兴	学	学	学

Composite capabilities: 1 2 3 4 5 6 7 8 9 10

prefix/phrase	suffix/phrase
study 学习 xuéxí	literature 文学 wénxué
school 学校 xuéxiào	chemistry 化学 huàxué
student 学生 xuéshēng	medical science 医学 yīxué
academic year 学年 xuénián	history studies 历史学 lìshǐxué
record of formal schooling 学历 xuélì	natural science 自然学 zìránxué

Ancient character

noun

Compound element
子 *child*

孩

Compound element
亥 *an interaction between two elements*

child

Note in Chinese

孩 = ♀ + 𠄎

左边是孩子（P169
子），右上是二，表
示两个人，"二"的
下面左是男，右是
女。组合后可能暗
示男女合欢，孩子
出生。

🔊 READ ALOUD

A CHILD is produced when the opposing energies of man and woman unite. CHILD is hái（孩）.

Stroke order

Composite capabilities: **1** 2 3 4 5 6 7 8 9 10

prefix/phrase	suffix/phrase
child 孩子 háizi	kids 小孩儿 xiǎoháir
childish 孩子气 háiziqì	
infancy 孩提 háití	

Ancient
character

verb
noun
adjective

Note in Chinese

练 = 纟 + 柬

Compound element

纟 *silk cocoon*

练

Compound element

柬 *boiler*

这是"練"的简
体。左边是丝，右
边是加热的器皿。
"练"做名词，是
丝绞合成的线；
后多用于动词，是
"练习"，可能因
为沸水里把茧抽出
丝来需要反复练习
的原因。

practice;
train; drill;
boil and scour
raw silk

white silk

experienced;
skilled

🔊 READ ALOUD

The technique of extracting silk from cocoons requires a lot of PRACTICE.
PRACTICE is liàn（练）.

Stroke order

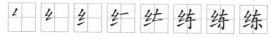

Composite capabilities: 1 2 3 4 5 6 7 8 9 10

prefix/phrase	suffix/phrase
practise characters 练字 liànzì	white silk 白练 báiliàn
practise 练习 liànxí	coach 教练 jiàoliàn
train troops 练兵 liànbīng	seasoned 老练 lǎoliàn

Ancient character

verb
preposition

Compound element

纟 *silk rope*

给

Compound element

合 *joint; cooperate*

Note in Chinese

给 = 纟 + 合

左边是丝，右上是容器的盖子，下面是口状的容器。上下扣在一起，表示有盖子的盒子。盒子有丝带装饰，可能用于馈赠，所以是"给"。

give
to; for

🔊 READ ALOUD

When GIVING presents, it was customary to tie boxes together with a silk ribbon. GIVE is gěi（给）.

Stroke order

Composite capabilities: 1 2 3 4 5 6 7 8 9 10

prefix/phrase	suffix/phrase
give sb. a way out 给出路 gěi chūlù	give as a present 送给 sònggěi
support 给力 gěilì	self-sufficient 自给自足 zìjǐzìzú

Ancient
character

| verb |
| noun |

Compound element		Compound element
马 *horse*		奇 *rare*
	骑	

| ride |
| horse or horse rider |

Note in Chinese

骑 = 馬 + 奇

这是"騎"的简
体。左边是马，右
上是一个人，他的
下面是鞍子。由于
有马在左边，所以
可以知道鞍子是放
在马背上的。

READ ALOUD

The first man to RIDE a horse must have had a rare kind of courage. RIDE
is qí（骑）.

Stroke order

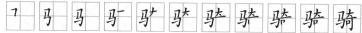

Composite capabilities: 1 2 3 4 5 6 7 8 9 10

prefix/phrase	suffix/phrase
ride a horse 骑马 qímǎ	saddle horse 坐骑 zuòqí
go by bicycle 骑车 qíchē	
horseman 骑手 qíshǒu	
unable to extricate oneself from a difficult situation 骑虎难下 qíhǔnánxià	

Ancient
character

Compound element

占 occupy

noun

verb

measure word

点

drop; spot; dot
stroke; point...

drip; check one
by one; light...

a bit; o'clock

Note in Chinese

点 = 占 + ⺀

这是"點"的简
体。下面的四个小
黑点是这个字古代
的意思。上面的部
分是一个物体，组
合后表示这个物体
会产生很多小的点
状体。

Compound element

⺀ *drop/dot*

🔊 READ ALOUD

A wooden spoon is used to stir this pot of soup. If it boiled over it would
run down the sides in little DROPLETS. DROP is diǎn（点）.

Stroke order

Composite capabilities: 1 2 3 4 5 6 7 8 9 10

prefix/phrase	suffix/phrase
order dishes 点菜 diǎncài	raindrop 雨点 yǔdiǎn
light a fire 点火 diǎnhuǒ	drink a bit of tea 喝一点儿茶
call the roll 点名 diǎnmíng	hē yìdiǎnr chá
	one o'clock 一点 yīdiǎn
	breakfast 早点 zǎodiǎn

Ancient character

Compound element

执 kneeled people and stretch arms

noun
adjective
verb

热

heat; fever; temperature

hot; warm hearted; popular

heat up

Compound element

灬 fire

Note in Chinese

热 = 𡗗 + 丸

这是"熱"的简体。左边是手臂，右边是跪在地上的人，下面是篝火。

🔊 READ ALOUD

People who lived in caves had to rely on HEAT from the fire to stay warm. HEAT is rè（热）.

Stroke order

Composite capabilities: 1 2 3 4 5 6 7 8 9 10

prefix/phrase	suffix/phrase
have deep love 热爱 rè'ài	scorching hot 炎热 yánrè
enthusiastic 热心 rèxīn	damp and hot 湿热 shīrè
hot days 热天 rètiān	
popular 热门 rèmén	
heat energy 热能 rènéng	

Ancient character

Compound element

food + dog

adjective *adverb* *conjunction*	然	*right; correct* *so; like that* *but; nevertheless; however*

Compound element

灬（火）fire

Note in Chinese

然 = 

左上边是生肉，右上边是一条狗，下面是篝火。自然是“道”，它的给予或不给予，永远都“对”。

READ ALOUD

Nature always knows the RIGHT thing to do to sustain life. It provides us with all that we need—fire, meat, even puppies! RIGHT is rán（然）.

Stroke order

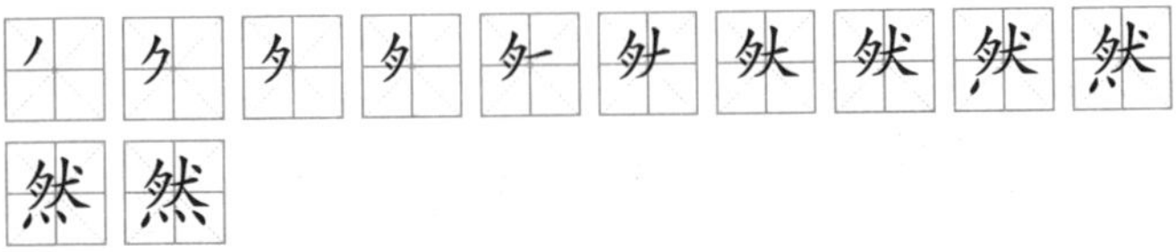

Composite capabilities: 1 2 3 4 5 6 7 8 9 10

prefix/phrase	suffix/phrase
but 然而 rán'ér	nature 自然 zìrán
then/after 然后 ránhòu	though/although 虽然 suīrán
however 然则 ránzé	suddenly 忽然 hūrán

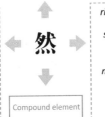

Ancient
character

Compound element

文 character

noun
adjective
verb
measure word

character;
script;
writing;
language;
literature;
culture

civil; gentle

cover

Compound element

Note in Chinese

文 = 𝖷

远古的中文大都刻
在坚硬的东西上，
所以笔画以直线为
主。

🕪 READ ALOUD

Ancient CHARACTERS were often carved onto hard surfaces so their
strokes tended to be in straight lines. CHARACTER is wén（文）.

Stroke order

Composite capabilities: 1 2 3 4 5 6 7 8 9 10

prefix/phrase	suffix/phrase
character 文字 wénzì	Chinese language 中文 Zhōngwén
scholar 文人 wénrén	English language 英文 Yīngwén
culture 文化 wénhuà	French language 法文 Fǎwén
civilization 文明 wénmíng	essay 论文 lùnwén
literature 文学 wénxué	

Ancient character

Compound element
ﾉ flames

noun
verb
adjective

火

fire; firearms; temper

lose one's temper

fiery; urgent

Compound element
人
tongues of fire

Note in Chinese

火 = ﾉ + 人

三个火舌组成一团火。

🔊 **READ ALOUD**

Three tongues of flames make a FIRE. FIRE is huǒ（火）.

Stroke order

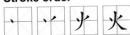

Composite capabilities: 1 2 3 4 5 6 7 8 **9** 10

prefix/phrase	suffix/phrase
volcano 火山 huǒshān	lose one's temper 发火 fāhuǒ
anger 火气 huǒqì	catch fire 起火 qǐhuǒ
fire disaster 火灾 huǒzāi	extinguish a fire 灭火 mièhuǒ
train 火车 huǒchē	

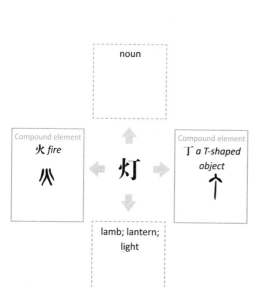

noun

Compound element
火 *fire*
从

灯

Compound element
丁 *a T-shaped object*
丁

lamb; lantern; light

Note in Chinese

灯 = 从 + 丁

这是"燈"的简体。左边是火（P180
火），右边是一个
"丁"字形的固定
装置。

READ ALOUD

Lanterns were lit with candles and hung from wooden stands. They were the prototypes of the modern LAMP. LAMP is dēng（灯）.

Stroke order

Composite capabilities: 1 2 3 4 5 6 7 8 9 10

prefix/phrase	suffix/phrase
the light of lamb 灯光 dēngguāng	electronic lamb 电灯 diàndēng
light holder 灯头 dēngtóu	street lamb 路灯 lùdēng

Ancient character

Compound element

心 heart

noun

心

heart; mind; feelings; intention; centre; core

Note in Chinese

心 =

"心"字就像人的心脏一样。

Compound element

🔊 **READ ALOUD**

This character is a pictogram of the human HEART. HEART is xīn（心）.

Stroke order

Composite capabilities: 1 2 3 4 5 6 7 8 9 10

prefix/phrase	suffix/phrase
loved 心爱 xīn'ài	warm hearted 热心 rèxīn
have an easy conscience 心安理得 xīn'ānlǐdé	disappointed 灰心 huīxīn
what one has learned from works 心得 xīndé	heart 内心 nèixīn
words in mind 心里话 xīnlǐhuà	
mentality 心理 xīnlǐ	

Ancient
character

adverb
verb

Compound element

心 *heart*

必

Compound element

ʃ *a sharp*
object

must;
certainly;
have to

Note in Chinese

必 = 𢖖 + ʃ
在 "心"（P182心）
中间有一个 "不可
忽略" 的信号。

● READ ALOUD

What is deeply carved in ones heart will CERTAINLY never be forgotten.
CERTAINLY is bì（必）.

Stroke order

Composite capabilities: 1 2 3 4 5 6 7 8 9 10

prefix/phrase	suffix/phrase
certainly 必定 bìdìng	may not 未必 wèibì
inevitable 必然 bìrán	no need 不必 búbì
must 必须 bìxū	

Ancient character

Compound element
田
brain/farmland

verb
noun

思

*think; consider;
think of*

thought; thinking

Compound element
心 heart

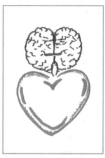

Note in Chinese

思 = 🧠 + 心

上面是人的脑子，
下面是心（P182
心）。思考的时
候，脑子要和心在
一起。孟子说：
"心之官则思。"

🔊 **READ ALOUD**

When we THINK of our friends, we often do so with both our heads and our hearts. THINK is sī（思）.

Stroke order

丿	冂	曰	甲	田	思	思	思	思

Composite capabilities: 1 2 3 4 5 6 7 8 9 10

prefix/phrase	suffix/phrase
thought 思想 sīxiǎng	think over 多思 duōsī
thinking 思考 sīkǎo	
way of thinking 思路 sīlù	

	Compound element **你** you	
noun	**您**	you (polite form)
	Compound element **心** heart	

Note in Chinese

您 = 你 + 心

你（P70你）在上，
心（P182心）在下：
从心里说"你好"
是表达尊重的"您
好"。

🔊 **READ ALOUD**

This student introduced YOU to the class with heartfelt sincerity and great respect. YOU is nín（您）.

Stroke order

丿　亻　亻　亻　亻　你　你　你　您　您　您

Composite capabilities: **1** 2 3 4 5 6 7 8 9 10

prefix/phrase	suffix/phrase
how do you do 您好 nínhǎo what's your surname 您贵姓 nín guìxìng please sit down 您请坐 nín qǐngzuò this telephone is for you 您的电话 nín de diànhuà	please come in 请您进来 qǐng nín jìnlái

Ancient
character

Compound element
相 photo/look

verb

想

*miss; think;
recall; suppose;
want to;
remember*

Note in Chinese

想 = 相 + 心

左上是树木（P192
木），右上是眼睛，
合起来是"看"；下
面是心（P182心）。
心"看"是想念。

Compound element
心 heat

🔊 **READ ALOUD**

When I MISS you, I can see you in my mind's eye. MISS is xiǎng（想）.

Stroke order

一	十	才	木	术	初	相	相	相	相

想	想	想

Composite capabilities: 1 2 3 4 5 6 7 8 9 10

prefix/phrase	suffix/phrase
idea 想法 xiǎngfǎ	thought 思想 sīxiǎng
image 想象 xiǎngxiàng	an ideal 理想 lǐxiǎng
homesick 想家 xiǎngjiā	
take things too hard 想不开	
xiǎngbukāi	
presumably 想必 xiǎngbì	

Ancient character

Compound element

户 window of house

noun ← 房 → *house; room*

Compound element

方 place/square

Note in Chinese

房 = 户 + 方

上边是窗户，下边是地方。有窗户的地方一定是房子。

🔊 **READ ALOUD**

In old villages, a square building with windows is usually somebody's HOUSE. HOUSE is fáng（房）.

Stroke order

Composite capabilities: 1 2 3 4 5 6 7 8 9 10

prefix/phrase	suffix/phrase
house 房子 fángzi	reception 门房 ménfáng
landlord 房东 fángdōng	kitchen 厨房 chúfáng
house property 房产 fángchǎn	bedroom 睡房 shuìfáng

Ancient
character

verb

Compound element
礻（示）
demonstrate

视

Compound element
见 *see*

see; look at;
regard; look
upon; inspect

Note in Chinese
视 = 礻 + 见

这是"视"的简
体。左边是天上来
的"神迹"，右边
是表示"观看"的
"见"（P218见）。

🔊 READ ALOUD

To have insight into the workings of nature is to SEE properly. SEE is
shì（视）.

Stroke order

Composite capabilities: 1 2 3 4 5 6 7 8 9 10

prefix/phrase	suffix/phrase
sight 视力 shìlì	television 电视 diànshì
angle of view 视角 shìjiǎo	ignore 无视 wúshì
seeing and hearing 视听 shìtīng	short-sighted 近视 jìnshì
sense of sight 视觉 shìjué	

Ancient
character

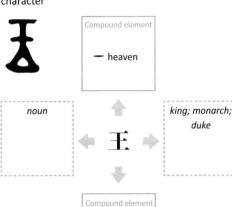

Compound element

一 heaven

noun

王

*king; monarch;
duke*

Compound element

二 earth and
person
丨 link

Note in Chinese

王 = 一 + 二 + 丨

三横分别代表
"天""人""地",
中间的一竖把三者
连在一起。组合表
明在中国的远古,
王权不可以继承,
那些能把天上的意
志传达到地上的人
被选为王。

🔊 **READ ALOUD**

The KING of China was considered a conduit between Heaven and Earth.
Only those chosen were allowed to fulfil this role. KING is wáng（王）.

Stroke order

Composite capabilities: 1 2 3 4 5 6 7 8 9 10

prefix/phrase	suffix/phrase
throne 王位 wángwèi	king of state 国王 guówáng
prince 王子 wángzǐ	duke 亲王 qīnwáng
the law of the land 王法 wángfǎ	Old Wang 老王 Lǎo Wáng
queen 王后 wánghòu	Young Wang 小王 Xiǎo Wáng
Mr. Wang 王先生	
Wáng xiānsheng	

Ancient character

verb

noun

Compound element
玉 = 王 + 、
jade

理

Compound element
里= 田+土
farmland + soil;
neighbourhood

manage;
put in order; pay
attention to
reason; logic;
natural science

Note in Chinese

理 = 王 + 、+里
左边是玉，右边
是表示有可耕的
"土"（P120土）即
"田"（P250田）。
"里"（P285里）是
居住地的名称。在古
代的乡里，人们把能
治玉的人视为会管理
的人。

☉ READ ALOUD

In the past, someone who could process jade would be considered a good MANAGER by the community. MANAGER is lǐ（理）.

Stroke order

Composite capabilities: 1 2 3 4 5 6 7 8 9 10

prefix/phrase	suffix/phrase
understand 理解 lǐjiě	reason 道理 dàolǐ
theory 理论 lǐlùn	physics 物理 wùlǐ
ideal 理想 lǐxiǎng	reasonable 有理 yǒulǐ
get haircut 理发 lǐfà	without reason 无理 wúlǐ

Ancient character

noun

Compound element

王 *jade stone*

Compound element

求 *demand/ fur/leather*

ball; globe; anything shaped like a ball; ball game; the globe

Note in Chinese

球 = 王 + 求

左边是玉，右边是求（P241求，捕抓的姿势）——据说中国远古的时候，为了训练战士的臂力和脚力，把玉石做成球再裹上皮毛让他们拼抢。

─ 🔊 **READ ALOUD** ─

The first BALLS used in sport were made of stones wrapped in leather to develop strong leg muscles. BALL is qiú（球）.

Stroke order

Composite capabilities: 1 2 **3** 4 5 6 7 8 9 10

prefix/phrase	suffix/phrase
star (of ball games) 球星 qiúxīng	football 足球 zúqiú
goal 球门 qiúmén	tennis 网球 wǎngqiú
gym shoes 球鞋 qiúxié	the globe 地球 dìqiú
round shape 球形 qiúxíng	the moon 月球 yuèqiú

Ancient character

Compound element

木 tree/wood

noun *adjective*

木

wood; tree; timber

made of wood; simple; wooden; numb

Compound element

Note in Chinese

木 = 𣎴

这是一个象形字，是天然的树干与树枝的样子。

🔊 READ ALOUD

This character resembles a tree with branches and a strong WOODEN trunk. WOOD is mù（木）.

Stroke order

Composite capabilities: 1 2 3 4 5 6 7 8 9 10

prefix/phrase	suffix/phrase
wood 木头 mùtou	trees 树木 shùmù
timber 木材 mùcái	flowers and trees 花木 huāmù
Jupiter 木星 Mùxīng	fruit tree 果木 guǒmù

Ancient
character

Compound element

木 tree

noun
adjective
adverb
measure word
verb

origin;
stem; basis;
native;
according to

Compound element

— ground

Note in Chinese

本 = 木 + 一

木（P192木）字的
下面一横是表示树
的根部，意为"树
之本"。

⊕ READ ALOUD

A tree's ORIGIN is in its roots, essential for absorbing nutrients from the
soil. ORIGIN is běn（本）.

Stroke order

Composite capabilities: 1 2 3 4 5 6 7 8 9 10

prefix/phrase	suffix/phrase
notebook 本子 běnzi	textbook 课本 kèběn
this year 本年 běnnián	notebook 练习本 liànxíběn
at first 本来 běnlái	cost 成本 chéngběn
	three books 三本书 sān běn shū

Ancient character

Compound element
木 tree

noun

李

plum; a Chinese surname

Compound element
子 child

Note in Chinese

李 = 木 + 子

上面是树木（P192
木），下面是一个
孩子（P169子）。
可能古代中国的果
树中，李子树上的
李子孩子最爱吃。

🎧 READ ALOUD

This child is standing under a PLUM tree, waiting for the ripened fruits to fall. PLUM is lǐ（李）.

Stroke order

Composite capabilities: 1 2 3 4 5 6 7 8 9 10

prefix/phrase	suffix/phrase
plum tree 李子树 lǐzishù	Old Li 老李 Lǎo Lǐ
plums 李子 lǐzi	have students everywhere
Mr. Li 李先生 Lǐ xiānsheng	桃李满天下 táolǐ mǎn tiānxià
Mrs. Li 李太太 Lǐ tàitai	

Ancient
character

	Compound element 夂 twig	
noun *measure word*	条	*twig; note; strip;* *item; order*
	Compound element 木 tree	

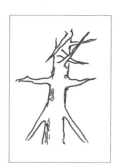

Note in Chinese

条 = 夂 + 木

这是"條"的简体。上边是杂枝，下面是树干（P192木）。

🔊 READ ALOUD

After a tree has died, the TWIGS can be used for firewood. TWIG is tiáo（条）.

Stroke order

Composite capabilities: 1 2 3 4 5 6 7 8 9 10

prefix/phrase	suffix/phrase
logic 条理 tiáolǐ	note 便条 biàntiáo
condition 条件 tiáojiàn	gold bar 金条 jīntiáo
note 条子 tiáozi	systematic 有条有理 yǒutiáoyǒulǐ

Ancient
character

Compound element
田 farmer's
field

果

noun
adverb
conjunction

fruit
really
if indeed
resolute

Compound element
木 tree

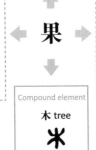

Note in Chinese

果 = 田 + 木

上面是田（P250
田），下面是木
（P192木）。果农
的田产不在地面而
在果树上。

🔊 READ ALOUD

FRUITS grow on trees just as crops grow in fields. FRUITS is guǒ（果）.

Stroke order

Composite capabilities: 1 2 3 4 5 6 7 8 9 10

prefix/phrase	suffix/phrase
fruit 果子 guǒzi	apple 苹果 píngguǒ
fruit tree 果树 guǒshù	fruits 水果 shuǐguǒ
fruit juice 果汁 guǒzhī	result 结果 jiéguǒ
as expected 果然 guǒrán	if 如果 rúguǒ

Ancient
character

noun
verb
measure word

Compound element
木 *tree*

根

艮 *changes
the meaning
to something
related*

root
completely

Note in Chinese

根 = 朩 + 𡰪

左边是木，右边是
艮；"艮"的加入
表达了与偏旁原义
（草本植物土上的
部分）相对的土下
部分"根"。

READ ALOUD

The ROOT of a tree is the part that reaches from the trunk into the
ground. ROOT is gēn（根）.

Stroke order

Composite capabilities: 1 2 3 4 5 6 7 8 9 10

prefix/phrase	suffix/phrase
basic 根本 gēnběn	root of the tree 树根 shùgēn
foundation 根基 gēnjī	
based on 根据 gēnjù	

Ancient character

noun

Compound element
木 *tree*

校

Compound element
交 *connect/make communicate*

school

Note in Chinese

校 = 木 + 交

左边是木，右边是表示连接或沟通的"交"。在古代，自然环境就是校园，其中对植物的了解是学校教学的内容之一。

🔊 **READ ALOUD**

For our ancestors, nature was their SCHOOL. Communicating with the environment taught them how to survive in the wild. SCHOOL is xiào（校）.

Stroke order

Composite capabilities: 1 2 3 4 5 6 7 8 9 10

prefix/phrase	suffix/phrase
principal 校长 xiàozhǎng	school 学校 xuéxiào
school uniform 校服 xiàofú	private school 私立校 sīlìxiào
school doctor 校医 xiàoyī	

Ancient
character

	noun	
Compound element 木 *wood/tree* 	椅	Compound element 奇 *rare*
	chair	

Note in Chinese

椅 = 木 + 奇

左边是木，右上是
一个人两腿分开，
右下是一个可以坐
的东西。

🍎 **READ ALOUD**

The oldest CHAIRS were made of wood, and people often sat astride
them for ease and comfort. CHAIR is yǐ（椅）.

Stroke order

椅　椅

Composite capabilities: 1 2 3 4 5 6 7 8 9 10

prefix/phrase	suffix/phrase
chair 椅子 yǐzi	wooden chair 木椅 mùyǐ
the back of a chair 椅背 yǐbèi	electric chair 电椅 diànyǐ
	armchair 沙发椅 shāfāyǐ

Ancient character

Compound element

吅 eyes

verb

哭

cry; weep; burst into tears

Compound element

犬 nose and mouth plus a drop of tears/dog

Note in Chinese

哭 =  + 

上面两个口表示是两只眼睛，下面的部分是鼻子和嘴，右边的一点是眼泪。

READ ALOUD

This character looks like a CRYING face, with a tear running down the corner of one eye. CRY is kū（哭）.

Stroke order

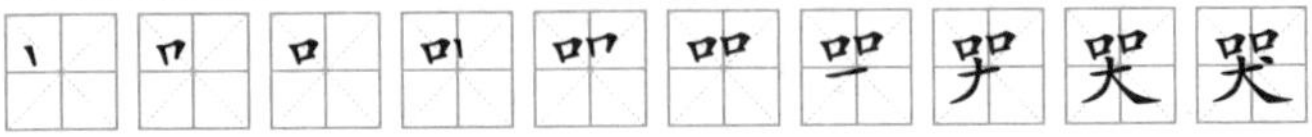

Composite capabilities: 1 2 3 4 5 6 7 8 9 10

prefix/phrase	suffix/phrase
complain tearfully 哭诉 kūsù	weep bitterly 痛哭 tòngkū
complain of being poverty 哭穷 kūqióng	cry 啼哭 tíkū
both funny and annoying 哭笑不得 kūxiàobùdé	
weep and wail 哭哭啼啼 kūkūtítí	

Ancient character

pronoun

Compound element
手 *hand*

我

Compound element
戈 *axe*

I; me; one; self; my

Note in Chinese

我 = 手 + 戈

这个字的左边的一半是手（P222手），右边的一半是一种叫"戈"的武器。远古时，人在外，必须手执武器以防身护己。

🌀 **READ ALOUD**

In ancient history, men seldom ventured out without a weapon in his hand so that he could protect himSELF from wild animals. I,ME or SELF is wǒ（我）.

Stroke order

Composite capabilities: 1 2 3 4 5 6 7 8 9 10

prefix/phrase	suffix/phrase
we 我们 wǒmen	myself 自我 zìwǒ
our country 我国 wǒguó	selfless 忘我 wàngwǒ
my family 我家 wǒjiā	

Ancient
character

noun
preposition
verb

Compound element

匕 *person*

比

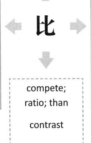

Compound element

匕 *person*

compete;
ratio; than

contrast

Note in Chinese

比 = 𠂉 + 𠂉
左右两边各是一个
人形。组合后表示
相比。

READ ALOUD

To compete is to COMPARE oneself against another. COMPARE is
bǐ（比）.

Stroke order

Composite capabilities: 1 2 3 4 5 6 7 8 9 10

prefix/phrase	suffix/phrase
ratio 比率 bǐlǜ	direct ratio 正比 zhèngbǐ
compare to him 比他 bǐ tā……	you compare to him 你和他比
compare 比较 bǐjiào	nǐ hé tā bǐ
	contrast 相比 xiāngbǐ

Ancient
character

Compound element

— the stop
line/hold

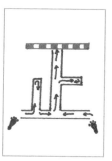

adjective
verb
adverb

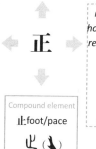

right; upright;
honest; standard;
regular; positive;
correct...

straiten;
correct...

just; right...

Compound element

止 foot/pace

止 (⻊)

Note in Chinese

正 = 一 + 止 (⻊)

下面是收住的脚
步，上面是一条界
线。组合后是提醒
人们，停下脚步，
思考后可以找到正
确的路径。

🔊 READ ALOUD

A road branching off is not necessarily a shortcut. It is best to pause
and consider which is the RIGHT path before proceeding. RIGHT is
zhèng（正）.

Stroke order

Composite capabilities: 1 2 3 4 5 6 7 8 9 10

prefix/phrase	suffix/phrase
justice 正义 zhèngyì	real 真正 zhēnzhèng
an action is in process of 正在 zhèngzài	stand at attention 立正 lìzhèng
front 正面 zhèngmiàn	
front door 正门 zhèngmén	
correct 正确 zhèngquè	

Ancient character

Compound element

止 foot

noun
measure word
verb

步

step; pace

walk

Compound element

foot

Note in Chinese

步 = +

上面是一只脚，下
面也是一只脚。两
脚之间，相差一
步。步也是动词，
如"步入前厅"。

🔊 READ ALOUD

To take a STEP, we have to place one foot in front of the other. STEP is
bù（步）.

Stroke order

| 丨 | 卜 | 止 | 止 | 半 | 步 | 步 |

Composite capabilities: 1 2 3 4 5 6 7 8 9 10

prefix/phrase	suffix/phrase
footstep 步子 bùzi	quick pace 快步 kuàibù
go on foot 步行 bùxíng	one step 一步 yí bù

Ancient
character

Compound element

日 sun

noun
adverb

日

sun; daytime;
day; time

daily

Note in Chinese

日 =

日是象形字，中间
的一横表示非常热。

Compound element

📣 READ ALOUD

The character looks like the SUN setting behind the horizon. SUN is
rì（日）.

Stroke order

Composite capabilities: 1 2 3 4 5 6 7 8 9 10

prefix/phrase	suffix/phrase
day 日子 rìzi	tomorrow 明日 míngrì
in the future 日后 rìhòu	Sunday 星期日 xīngqīrì
diary 日记 rìjì	working day 工作日 gōngzuòrì
calendar 日历 rìlì	holiday 假日 jiàrì
daily necessities 日用 rìyòng	
Japan 日本 Rìběn	

Ancient character

Compound element

⊙ sun

noun
adjective
adverb

早

morning
early
long ago

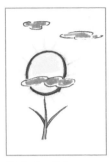

Note in Chinese

早 = ⊙ + 丫

上面是日（P205
日），下面是草。
显示了日出时的情
景。

Compound element

丫 grass

🔊 READ ALOUD

The MORNING Sun warms this tiny blade of grass, helping it to grow big and strong. MORNING is zǎo（早）.

Stroke order

Composite capabilities: 1 2 3 **4** 5 6 7 8 9 10

prefix/phrase	suffix/phrase
good morning 早上好 zǎoshang hǎo	morning call 叫早 jiàozǎo
breakfast 早点 zǎodiǎn	from morning till night 从早到晚
morning tea 早茶 zǎochá	cóng zǎo dào wǎn
sooner or later 早晚 zǎowǎn	
one's early years 早年 zǎonián	
for a long time 早已 zǎoyǐ	

Ancient
character

noun
adjective
adverb

Compound element

日 *sunlight*

○

时

Compound element

degree/measure

time; times;
season;
opportunity

current

now and then;
from time to
time

Note in Chinese

时 = ○ + 㞢

这 是 "時" 的 简
体。左边是日，右
边是长度的基本单
位 "寸"。古代用
日晷计时。

🕪 READ ALOUD

People used to tell TIME by measuring the arc of the shadow on the
sundial. TIME is shí（时）.

Stroke order

Composite capabilities: 1 2 3 4 5 6 7 8 9 10

prefix/phrase	suffix/phrase
time 时间 shíjiān	nine o'clock 九时 jiǔshí
(the duration of) time 时候 shíhou	normally 平时 píngshí
current events 时事 shíshì	on time 按时 ànshí
often 时时 shíshí	all the time 无时无刻 wú shí wú kè
jet lag 时差 shíchā	

Ancient character

adjective
noun
verb

Compound element
日 *sun*

明

Compound element
月 *moon*

Note in Chinese

明 = 日 + 月

左边是日，右边是月（P230月）。太阳和月亮同时在天空，很明亮。

bright; clear; open; honest

tomorrow; sight

understand

✿ READ ALOUD

When the sun and the moon are together in the sky, the evening would be BRIGHTER than usual. BRIGHT is míng（明）.

Stroke order

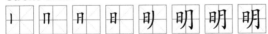

Composite capabilities: 1 2 3 4 5 6 7 8 9 10

prefix/phrase	suffix/phrase
bright 明亮 míngliàng	smart 聪明 cōngmíng
tomorrow 明天 míngtiān	indicate 说明 shuōmíng
celebrity 明星 míngxīng	make known 表明 biǎomíng
be clear about 明了 míngliǎo	enlightened 开明 kāimíng
know well 明知 míngzhī	

Ancient character

Compound element
日 sun

verb adjective	易	change; exchange — easy; amiable

Compound element
勿 no more

Note in Chinese

易 = ㊀ + ⟋

上面是日（P205 日）光，下面是表示日光"没有"或"不存在"了。组合后的含义是"易"——变易。这是中国阴阳学说的重要理念。

🔊 READ ALOUD

As the sun sets, it casts an ever CHANGING shadow on the land. CHANGING is yì（易）.

Stroke order

丨	冂	日	日	月	月	易	易

Composite capabilities: 1 2 3 4 5 6 7 8 9 10

prefix/phrase	suffix/phrase
the Book of Changes 易经 Yìjīng	easy 容易 róngyì
change hands 易手 yìshǒu	trade 贸易 màoyì
be easy to 易于 yìyú	simple and easy 简易 jiǎnyì

Ancient character

Compound element

三 + 人
sky, earth and people

noun

春

spring; love; life

Compound element

日 sun

Note in Chinese

春 = 三 + 人 + 日

上面的三横表示"天""地"。中间是一个"人"字贯穿，下面是太阳（P205日），组合后表达太阳从地底下温暖世界，这时正是春天。

🔊 READ ALOUD

The sun nourishes the earth and life begins to stir. It is SPRING! SPRING is chūn（春）.

Stroke order

Composite capabilities: 1 2 3 4 **5** 6 7 8 9 10

prefix/phrase	suffix/phrase
spring 春天 chūntiān spring breeze 春风 chūnfēng Chinese New Year 春节 Chūnjié	youth 青春 qīngchūn

Ancient character

Compound element

日 sun

adjective
verb

是

correct; right

to be;
be just right

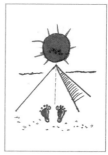

Note in Chinese

是 = ☉ + 止 + 一

上面是太阳（P205
日），下面是脚步
在 适 度 的 线 上 停
住。组合后表示此
时太阳正好直射，
正确!

Compound element

（止 + 一）＝正

 + 一

foot at the line =
correct

🎙 READ ALOUD

When the sun is overhead at midday, people pause to contemplate its positive energy and say 'YES' to life. YES is shì（是）.

Stroke order

Composite capabilities: 1 2 3 4 5 6 7 8 9 10

prefix/phrase	suffix/phrase
right or wrong 是非 shìfēi	not correct 不是 búshì
is that right 是吗 shì ma	yes indeed 就是 jiùshì
yes or no 是不是 shì búshì	only is 才是 cáishì
that's it 是的 shì de	only 只是 zhǐshì

Ancient character

Compound element
日 stars

noun

星

star; bit

Note in Chinese

星 = ° ° ° + 丫

上面是与日（P205日）俱来的星球，下面是地球上的生（P22生）命。古体字形显示，那时没有污染，繁星环绕并照耀着万物苍生。

Compound element

丫
earth/land

⚙ **READ ALOUD**

There are countless STARS in the sky, but only one is visible through the polluted air. STAR is xīng（星）.

Stroke order

丶 丨冂 冂日 日旦 旦旦 旦旦 旦旦 星

Composite capabilities: 1 2 3 4 **5** 6 7 8 9 10

prefix/phrase	suffix/phrase
stars 星星 xīngxing	Mars 火星 Huǒxīng
planets 星球 xīngqiú	Mercury 水星 Shuǐxīng
star space 星空 xīngkōng	celebrity 明星 míngxīng
Sunday 星期天 xīngqītiān	film star 影星 yǐngxīng

Ancient
character

noun
adjective

Compound element

日 *sun*

晚

Compound element

免 *excuse/*
without

evening; night;
late; younger

Note in Chinese

晚 = 日 + 免

左边是日，右边
原字是"安"，
表示平静、安好
等意。现在右文是
"免"，组合后表
示太阳不存在，所
以是晚。

☀ READ ALOUD

The sun disappearing behind the horizon signals the onset of EVENING. It is bedtime for little rabbits! EVENING is wǎn（晚）.

Stroke order

Composite capabilities: 1 2 3 4 5 6 7 8 9 10

prefix/phrase	suffix/phrase
evening 晚上 wǎnshang	evening 夜晚 yèwǎn
good night 晚安 wǎn'ān	at dusk 傍晚 bàngwǎn
to be late 晚了 wǎnle	sooner or later 早晚 zǎowǎn
one's later age 晚年 wǎnnián	
evening papers 晚报 wǎnbào	

Ancient character

Compound element
並 two people to share

adjective

普

universal; general

Compound element
日 sunny

Note in Chinese

普 = 並 + ☉

上面是两个人并肩而立，下面是太阳（P205 日）。这个组合是表示"天德普照"。

🔊 READ ALOUD

The sun's gift of warmth and energy is UNIVERSAL, reaching everyone equally and without bias. UNIVERSAL is pǔ（普）.

Stroke order

Composite capabilities: 1 2 3 4 5 6 7 8 9 10

prefix/phrase	suffix/phrase
ordinary 普通 pǔtōng	dissemination of science
Mandarin 普通话 Pǔtōnghuà	科普 kēpǔ
illuminate all things 普照 pǔzhào	
general election 普选 pǔxuǎn	

Ancient
character

Compound element

月 hat

adverb

最

most

Note in Chinese

最 = 冃 + 臥

上面是帽子，左下是
耳（P272耳）朵，右
下是手执利器。组合
后意思之一是表示最
极端的战争行为是把
敌人的耳朵割下来做
战利品。

Compound element

取 = 耳 + 手
take=ear + hand

臥 = ৎ + ㇏

READ ALOUD

The MOST extreme practice in war was to cut off the enemy's ear as a
show of strength. MOST is zuì（最）.

Stroke order

丶	冂	冃	日	旦	旱	昗	昗	昗	冐

冐	最

Composite capabilities: 1 2 3 4 5 6 7 8 9 10

prefix/phrase	suffix/phrase
biggest 最大 zuì dà	
best 最好 zuì hǎo	
final 最后 zuìhòu	
recently 最近 zuìjìn	
up-to-date 最新 zuì xīn	

Ancient character

noun

Note in Chinese

影 = 景 + 彡

左上是日（P205 日），下面是高大的庙宇，右文是表示阴影的三撇。组合后意为"影子"。

Compound element

景 *sunlight* + *capital*= *landscape*

影

Compound element

彡 *shadow*

shadow; reflection; trace; photograph; film

🔊 **READ ALOUD**

Sunlight falling on a building will create different SHADOWS at different hours of the day. SHADOW is yǐng（影）.

Stroke order

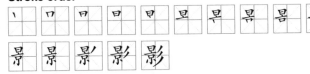

Composite capabilities: 1 2 **3** 4 5 6 7 8 9 10

prefix/phrase	suffix/phrase
shadow 影子 yǐngzi	film 电影 diànyǐng
film and TV 影视 yǐngshì	take a group photo 合影 héyǐng
cinema 影院 yǐngyuàn	shoot a film 摄影 shèyǐng
album 影集 yǐngjí	inverted reflection in water 倒影 dàoyǐng

Ancient
character

Compound element

two hands
are holding a
stick

adjective

贵

*expensive; highly
valued; of high
rank*

Note in Chinese

贵 =

这是"贵"的简体。
古体字上面的部分是
两只手抓着一物；下
面是古代的"贝壳
币"；意思是把物价
拔高了。

Compound element

贝 money or
business

🐟 READ ALOUD

Most people go to the market early as it is more EXPENSIVE to shop in
the middle of the day. EXPENSIVE is guì（贵）.

Stroke order

Composite capabilities: 1 2 3 4 5 6 7 8 9 10

prefix/phrase	suffix/phrase
honoured guest 贵客 guìkè	quite expensive 很贵 hěn guì
surname(polite way for question) 贵姓 guìxìng	famous and precious 名贵 mínguì
precious 贵重 guìzhòng	

Ancient character

Compound element

目 eye

verb
noun

见

see; watch; meet with; appear to be; refer to

view; opinion

Compound element

儿 two legs

Note in Chinese

见 = + 丿

这是"見"的简体。上面是目（眼睛）；下面是身体与两条腿。眼睛长在身体的最高部位，其作用是"见"。

🔊 **READ ALOUD**

This ant's eyes are placed high on his head so he can SEE further. SEE is jiàn（见）.

Stroke order

   见

Composite capabilities: 1 2 3 4 5 6 7 8 9 10

prefix/phrase	suffix/phrase
meet 见面 jiànmiàn	meet with 会见 huìjiàn
experience 见识 jiànshi	opinion 意见 yìjiàn
learn on the job 见习 jiànxí	foresee 预见 yùjiàn
witness 见证 jiànzhèng	preconceived opinion
view 见解 jiànjiě	成见 chéngjiàn

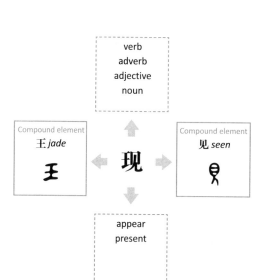

Note in Chinese

现 = 王 + 見

左边是玉，右文是
见（P218见）。
合起来表示玉在某
处显现；而第一个
见到玉的，是发现
者。不过，古字的
"见"与"现"是
同一个字。

─ 🐞 READ ALOUD ─

When the mellow beauty of jade first APPEARED in front of human eyes
it must have been a pleasant surprise! APPEAR is xiàn（现）.

Stroke order

| 一 | 二 | 于 | 王 | 珇 | 玏 | 珼 | 现 |

Composite capabilities: 1 2 3 4 5 6 7 8 9 10

prefix/phrase	suffix/phrase
appear 现出 xiànchū	achieve 实现 shíxiàn
phenomenon 现象 xiànxiàng	show 体现 tǐxiàn
reality 现实 xiànshí	perform 表现 biǎoxiàn
now 现在 xiànzài	
this life 现世 xiànshì	

Ancient character

Compound element

覺 gain knowledge

noun
verb

觉

sleep
sense; feel;
wake up; awake;
become aware

Note in Chinese

觉 = 學 + 見

这是"覺"的简体。
上面的三竖表示脑
子里的各种思维活
动。中间是屋顶，
下面是见（P218
见）。组合起来表
达思索与见识之间
要有"觉"。

Compound element

见 see/meet

見

🌀 **READ ALOUD**

When we SLEEP, our dreams can often offer us the best insights,
inspiration and creativity. SLEEP is jiào（觉）.

Stroke order

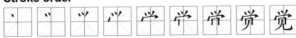

Composite capabilities: 1 2 3 4 5 6 7 8 9 10

prefix/phrase	suffix/phrase
feel 觉得 juéde	be conscious 自觉 zìjué
awareness 觉悟 juéwù	sense of hearing 听觉 tīngjué
awaken 觉醒 juéxǐng	vision 视觉 shìjué
detect 觉察 juéchá	sleep 睡觉 shuìjiào

Ancient character

Compound element

牛 ox

noun
adjective

牛

ox; cattle

stubborn

Compound element

Note in Chinese

牛 = ♆

古体字的牛还是两
只牛角并存，后来
变体，右边的角去
掉了。

🔊 **READ ALOUD**

This character looks like a BULL but with one horn missing! BULL is niú（牛）.

Stroke order

Composite capabilities: 1 2 3 4 5 6 7 8 9 10

prefix/phrase	suffix/phrase
beef 牛肉 niúròu	cow 奶牛 nǎiniú
milk 牛奶 niúnǎi	buffalo 水牛 shuǐniú
ox horn 牛角 niújiǎo	rhinoceros 犀牛 xīniú
beef steak 牛排 niúpái	

Ancient character

Compound element

手 hand

noun
adjective
adverb
measure word

手

hand
handy
personally

Note in Chinese

手 = 手

这是一只手的象形图。但是与其他部分组合且位置在左边时，变成"扌"这个偏旁。

Compound element

🔊 **READ ALOUD**

There are five fingers on each HAND. HAND is shǒu（手）.

Stroke order

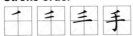

Composite capabilities: 1 2 3 4 5 6 7 8 9 10

prefix/phrase	suffix/phrase
mobile 手机 shǒujī	handle 把手 bǎshǒu
wristwatch 手表 shǒubiǎo	stop 住手 zhùshǒu
handbook 手册 shǒucè	do fine 得手 déshǒu
handwork 手工 shǒugōng	

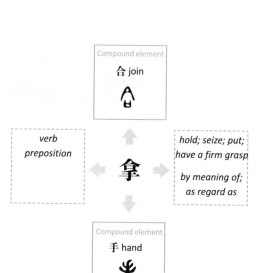

Compound element
合 join

verb
preposition

拿

hold; seize; put;
have a firm grasp

by meaning of;
as regard as

Compound element
手 hand

Note in Chinese

拿 = 合 + 手

上面是一个合，像
一个有盖子的盒
子，意思是合作；
下面是手（P222
手），五指合作才
能拿东西。这个字
本来与"奴"是一
个字，有强制的意
思。

☞ READ ALOUD

To HOLD an object we have to close our fingers. HOLD is ná（拿）.

Stroke order

Composite capabilities: 1 2 3 4 5 6 7 8 9 10

prefix/phrase	suffix/phrase
hold object 拿东西 ná dōngxi	massage 推拿 tuīná
take away 拿开 nákāi	arrest 捉拿 zhuōná
expert 拿手 náshǒu	
can manage 拿得起来 ná de qǐlái	

Ancient
character

Compound element

气 air

Note in Chinese

气 = 气

这 是 "氣" 的 简
体。很接近古体，
更像沿着山体飘忽
不定的 "气"。

noun
verb

气

air; gas; breath;
smell; weather;
airs; manner;
spirit; insult

get angry;
annoy

Compound element

- 🔊 **READ ALOUD** -

AIR is in constant flow and motion. AIR is qì（气）.

Stroke order

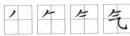

Composite capabilities: 1 2 3 4 5 6 7 8 9 10

prefix/phrase	suffix/phrase
gas 气体 qìtǐ	air 空气 kōngqì
climate 气候 qìhòu	atmosphere 大气 dàqì
	get angry 生气 shēngqì
	fortune 运气 yùnqi
	natural gas 天然气 tiānránqì

Ancient character

adjective
verb
noun

Compound element
⺕ hand
+
目 ear

敢

Compound element
攵 tool

dare
courage
brave

Note in Chinese

敢 = ⺕ + 目 + 攵

左边是一只被从上面揪住的耳（P272 耳）朵；右文是一把刀。这种残酷的表示勇敢的行为在世界各地都有。

⚡ READ ALOUD

It took a DARING man to cut off his enemy's ear on the battlefield! DARE is gǎn（敢）.

Stroke order

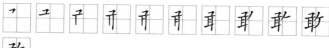

Composite capabilities: 1 2 3 4 5 6 7 8 9 10

prefix/phrase	suffix/phrase
dare to 敢于 gǎnyú	brave 勇敢 yǒnggǎn
	courageous and resolute
	果敢 guǒgǎn

Ancient character

verb
noun

Compound element

math +
child

Compound element
攵 *tool/method*

Note in Chinese

教 = 𡥀 + 孑 + 攵

左上是土（P120土）地，左下是孩子（P169子），长长的一撇是教具。右文也是教具，可能是生产工具。远古教习的理念大多是人如何与自然相处。

teach; instruct; educate

religion

READ ALOUD

To TEACH our children well is to plant good seeds in their hearts. TEACH is jiāo（教）.

Stroke order

Composite capabilities: 1 2 3 4 5 6 7 8 9 10

prefix/phrase	suffix/phrase
teaching math 教数学 jiāo shùxué	Taoism 道教 Dàojiào
education 教育 jiàoyù	Confucian 儒教 Rújiào
teacher 教师 jiàoshī	religion 宗教 zōngjiào
coach 教练 jiàoliàn	
church 教会 jiàohuì	

verb
noun

Compound element
米+女
corns + woman

数

Compound element
攵 *tool*

Note in Chinese

数 = 米 + 女 + 攵

这 是 " 数 " 的 简
体。左上是米（P269
米 ） ， 左 下 是 女
（P163 女）子；右
文 " 攵 " 是 计 算 的
工具。

shǔ: count;
be reckoned;
numerate; list

shù: number;
figure

several; a few

- ✿ READ ALOUD

Women used to rely on the abacus to keep COUNT of the household
expenditure, making sure there is enough corn to feed the family. COUNT
is shǔ（数）.

Stroke order

| 丶 | 丶丶 | 丷 | 半 | 半 | 米 | 米 | 娄 | 娄 | 娄 |

| 娄 | 数 | 数 |

Composite capabilities: 1 2 3 4 5 6 7 8 9 10

prefix/phrase	suffix/phrase
count 数数 shǔshù	countless 无数 wúshù
rank very high 数一数二 shǔyīshǔ'èr	odd 奇数 jīshù
mathematics 数学 shùxué	even 偶数 ǒushù
number 数字 shùzì	

Ancient character

adjective
adverb

Compound element
亲
close/in person

新

Compound element
斤 *axe*

new; fresh;
up-to-date;
brand new

newly; recently

Note in Chinese

新 = 亲 + 斤

左上是小树刚刚顶出的新芽（P242 立），左下是树干（P192木）。右文是一把修剪树枝的工具。

✿ READ ALOUD

When NEW leaves sprout from a young tree it is important to tend it carefully. NEW is xīn（新）.

Stroke order

Composite capabilities: 1 2 3 4 5 6 7 8 9 10

prefix/phrase	suffix/phrase
new students 新学生 xīn xuésheng	brand new 全新 quánxīn
new cloths 新衣服 xīn yīfu	love the new and loathe the old
new property 新房 xīnfáng	喜新厌旧 xǐxīnyànjiù
bride 新娘 xīnniáng	
new hand 新手 xīnshǒu	
news 新闻 xīnwén	

Ancient
character

Compound element

罒 + 冖
hands + roof

noun
verb

愛

love;
affection;
be fond of

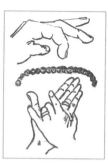

Note in Chinese

爱 ＝ ⻌ ＋ 冖 ＋ 友

这 是 " 爱 " 的 简
体 。 顶 上 是 呵 护 的
手 指 ， 中 间 是 屋
顶 ， 下 面 是 两 只 紧
握 的 手 。

Compound element

友 two hands
joined together

- 🔊 READ ALOUD -

Your friend must LOVE you very much if he is willing to lend you a hand
with the construction of your house! LOVE is ài（爱）.

Stroke order

Composite capabilities: 1 2 3 4 5 6 7 8 9 10

prefix/phrase	suffix/phrase
hobby 爱好 àihào	maternal love 母爱 mǔài
treasure 爱护 àihù	lovely 可爱 kě'ài
lover 爱人 àirén	

Ancient character

noun
adjective

Compound element

月 *moon/body*

月

Compound element

moon; month

full-month-
shaped

Note in Chinese

月 = 〉

月是象形字，月亮
像是被一片云遮住
了一点。

⚙ READ ALOUD

The beauty of the MOON is here enhanced by the presence of a light mist. MOON is yuè（月）.

Stroke order

   月

Composite capabilities: 1 2 3 4 5 6 7 8 9 10

prefix/phrase	suffix/phrase
moon 月亮 yuèliang	January 一月 Yīyuè
moonlight 月光 yuèguāng	crescent 新月 xīnyuè
month 月份 yuèfèn	a new baby is one month old 满月
monthly income 月薪 yuèxīn	mǎnyuè
moon cake 月饼 yuèbing	

Ancient character

Compound element
ヨ arm/hand

verb

有

have; there is; exist

Compound element

ℙ meat

Note in Chinese

有 = ヨ + ℙ

上面是手臂，下面
是肉，组合后表示
拥有。

⚙ **READ ALOUD**

It is lovely to HAVE a hot sausage on a cold night! HAVE is yǒu（有）.

Stroke order

一 ナ 才 有 有 有

Composite capabilities: 1 2 3 4 5 6 7 8 9 10

prefix/phrase	suffix/phrase
have property 有房子 yǒu fángzi	do not have 没有 méiyǒu
have skill 有能力 yǒu nénglì	now have 现有 xiànyǒu
relate to 有关 yǒuguān	will have 将有 jiāng yǒu
reasonable 有理 yǒulǐ	

Ancient
character

verb
noun

Compound element
舟 *boat*
ﾖ

服

Compound element
Ᏸ
obeyed person
X *force*
Ᏸ+X =serve

Note in Chinese

服 = ﾖ + ᏰX

左边是一条船，右
文像一个人被力所
屈从的样子。

obey; serve;
drink(medicine)

clothes

⚙ READ ALOUD

Slaves were often forced onto boats to work hard and OBEY orders. OBEY
is fú（服）.

Stroke order

丿	月	月	月	月	月	服	服

Composite capabilities: 1 2 3 4 5 6 7 8 9 10

prefix/phrase	suffix/phrase
obey 服从 fúcóng	cloths 衣服 yīfu
serve 服务 fúwù	comfortable 舒服 shūfu
submit to the law 服法 fúfǎ	
take medicine 服药 fúyào	

Ancient
character

noun
verb

Compound element
月 *body/feather*

朋

Compound element
月 *body/feather*

Note in Chinese

朋 = 夕 + 夕

左是表示"身体",
右边也是,两个很
相似,所以可做朋
友。

friend

join together;
gang up

🐦 **READ ALOUD**

Birds love to pair up with their FRIENDS when they fly. FRIEND is
péng(朋).

Stroke order

Composite capabilities: 1 2 3 4 5 6 7 8 9 10

prefix/phrase	suffix/phrase
friend 朋友 péngyou	relatives and friends 亲朋 qīnpéng
act in collusion 朋比为奸	guests 宾朋 bīnpéng
péngbǐwéijiān	

Ancient character

Compound element

古 baby

verb

育

raise; cultivate;
give birth;
educate; nourish

Note in Chinese

育 = 古 + 月

上面是一个头朝母
亲的幼儿，下面是
母亲的乳房。组合
后表示孩子是母亲
用奶水养育的。

Compound element

月 breast

🔊 READ ALOUD

A baby is NOURISHED by his mother's milk as well as her constant care.
NOURISH is yù（育）.

Stroke order

Composite capabilities: 1 **2** 3 4 5 6 7 8 9 10

prefix/phrase	suffix/phrase
educate 育人 yùrén	moral education 德育 déyù
breeding 育种 yùzhǒng	intellectual education 智育 zhìyù
raise children 育儿 yù'ér	sports 体育 tǐyù

Ancient
character

adjective

Compound element
月 *meat/body*

胖

Compound element
半 *a half*

Note in Chinese

胖 = 月 + 半
左边是身体，右文
是一个"半"（P55
半）字，组合后表
示这个人的体重是
普通人的一个半。

fat; fatty

🔊 READ ALOUD

A person is considered overweight if half his body is made up of FAT! FAT
is pàng（胖）.

Stroke order

Composite capabilities: 1 2 3 4 5 6 7 8 9 10

prefix/phrase	suffix/phrase
a fat person 胖子 pàngzi plump 胖乎乎 pànghūhū	small fatty 小胖子 xiǎopàngzi

Ancient character

noun adjective verb	

Compound element

月 *bear's body*

能

Compound element

paws

ability; skill;
energy

able; capable

can; be able to

Note in Chinese

能 = + ｆ ｆ

左上是一只熊头，下面是它的身体，右边是爪子。组合后表示熊有很强的体能。

🎧 READ ALOUD

A bear has the ABILITY to kill another animal with his claws. ABILITY is néng（能）.

Stroke order

     育 育

Composite capabilities: 1 2 3 4 5 6 7 8 9 10

prefix/phrase	suffix/phrase
capability 能力 nénglì	all-powerful 全能 quánnéng
energy resources 能源 néngyuán	maybe 可能 kěnéng
expert 能手 néngshǒu	physical power 体能 tǐnéng
able 能干 nénggàn	skills 技能 jìnéng
able person 能人 néngrén	

Ancient character

noun

月 *body*

脚

去 *leave*+ 卩 *seal*

foot; base

Note in Chinese

脚 = 月 + 去 + 卩

左边表示身体的一部分，中间是"离开"的去（P82 去），右边是腿跪地。这是后起的字，可解释为身体接触与离开地面的部位是"脚"。

· 🔊 READ ALOUD ·

When we walk we leave prints which bear the shape of our FEET. FOOT is jiǎo（脚）。

Stroke order

ノ	月	月	月	肝	肝	胖	脉	脏	脚	脚

Composite capabilities: 1 2 3 4 5 6 7 8 9 10

prefix/phrase	suffix/phrase
pace 脚步 jiǎobù	bound foot 小脚 xiǎojiǎo
toe 脚趾 jiǎozhǐ	ability to walk 腿脚 tuǐjiǎo
heel 脚跟 jiǎogēn	
strength of one's legs 脚力 jiǎolì	

Ancient
character

Compound element

sky and cloud

noun
verb

风

wind; practice;
custom; style

rumoured;
unfounded

Note in Chinese

风 = ∩ + X

这是"风"的简
体。拱起的部分是
大气层，里面的X表
示有变化。组合后
是大气有变化。

Compound element

X danger   **川** river

🔊 READ ALOUD

The weather forecast warns of big storms with high WINDS. WIND is
fēng（风）.

Stroke order

Composite capabilities: 1 2 3 4 5 6 7 8 9 10

prefix/phrase	suffix/phrase
wind force 风力 fēnglì	gale 大风 dàfēng
wind and rain 风雨 fēngyǔ	north wind 北风 běifēng
local tradition and customs	academic atmosphere
风土 fēngtǔ	学风 xuéfēng
geomantic omen 风水 fēngshuǐ	
general mood 风气 fēngqì	

Ancient
character

noun
measure word

Compound element

 water

水

Compound element

water; river;
waters; a liquid

Note in Chinese

水 =

这个字的字形就像
陆地上蜿蜒流淌的
河流，所以是水。

🔊 READ ALOUD

WATER from a river often flows round small islands before it enters the sea. WATER is shuǐ（水）.

Stroke order

Composite capabilities: 1 2 3 4 5 6 7 8 9 **10**

prefix/phrase	suffix/phrase
water transportation 水路 shuǐlù	river waters 河水 héshuǐ
waterpower 水力 shuǐlì	lake waters 湖水 húshuǐ
standard 水平 shuǐpíng	seawater 海水 hǎishuǐ
seaman 水手 shuǐshǒu	ice water 冰水 bīngshuǐ
natural environment and climate 水土 shuǐtǔ	sparking water 汽水 qìshuǐ
paddy field 水田 shuǐtián	

Ancient
character

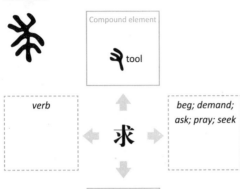

Compound element

彐 tool

verb

求

beg; demand;
ask; pray; seek

Compound element

氺 fur/tail

Note in Chinese

求 = 彐 + 氺

上部是手，中间与
下部是动物尾部。
古人为求暖而杀死
动物，取它们的皮
毛做裘衣。为此，
祈求神明的宽恕。

🐾 **READ ALOUD**

Before killing animals for their meat or fur, our ancestors would first BEG
their forgiveness with prayer. BEG is qiú（求）.

Stroke order

Composite capabilities: 1 2 3 4 5 6 7 8 9 10

prefix/phrase	suffix/phrase
ask for help 求人 qiúrén	demand 要求 yāoqiú
seek survival 求生 qiúshēng	request 请求 qǐngqiú
go to school 求学 qiúxué	respond to every plea 有求必应
seek knowledge 求知 qiúzhī	yǒuqiúbìyìng

Ancient character

Compound element ↓ grass/grow	

pronoun adverb	每	every; each; per; each time on each occasion; often

Compound element
母
Mum/breast

Note in Chinese

每 = ↓ + 身

字 的 顶 上 是 小 草 生
长 的 样 子 ，下 面 是
母 亲 在 给 孩 子 喂
奶 。组 合 后 表 明 每
个 孩 子 都 是 由 母 亲
每 日 喂 养 长 大 的 ，
如 同 小 草 生 长 。

─ 🔊 **READ ALOUD** ─

EVERY baby who is nourished by his mother's milk has the chance of growing healthy and strong. EVERY is měi（每）.

Stroke order

ノ	⌐	ⱡ	毎	每	每	每

Composite capabilities: 1 2 3 4 5 6 7 8 9 10

prefix/phrase	suffix/phrase
each day 每天 měitiān	often 每每 měiměi
everyone 每人 měirén	
at all times 每时每刻 měishíměikè	

Ancient
character

Compound element

adult

verb
adjective
adverb

立

stand; erect;
set; establish;
conclude

upright; erect

immediately

Compound element

一 ground

Note in Chinese

立 = 𠆢 + 一

这个字形就是一个
人张开两臂、保持
平衡地站立着。

🎧 **READ ALOUD**

It is easier to STAND on a skateboard with arms outstretched for balance.
STAND is lì（立）.

Stroke order

Composite capabilities: 1 2 3 4 5 6 7 8 9 10

prefix/phrase	suffix/phrase
base oneself upon 立足 lìzú	standing 站立 zhànlì
make laws 立法 lìfǎ	establish 设立 shèlì
the Beginning of Spring 立春 lìchūn	build up 建立 jiànlì
halt 立定 lìdìng	
three dimensional 立体 lìtǐ	
immediately 立即 lìjí	

Ancient
character

Compound element
亲 tree grows
bud

adjective
noun
adverb
verb

亲

dear; close

parents;
marriage;
relatives; bride

in person

kiss

Compound element

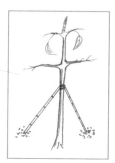

Note in Chinese

亲 =

字 的 上 部 是 初 立
（P242立）在顶上的
新芽，下边是树干
（P192木）。树干与
枝叶是母子关系，所
以亲。

🔊 **READ ALOUD**

New buds are as DEAR to a tree as a child is to his family. DEAR is
qīn（亲）.

Stroke order

Composite capabilities: 1 2 3 4 **5** 6 7 8 9 10

prefix/phrase	suffix/phrase
dear 亲爱 qīn'ài close 亲近 qīnjìn personally 亲自 qīnzì intimate 亲热 qīnrè relatives and good friends 亲朋好友 qīnpénghǎoyǒu as dear to each other as members of one family 亲如一家 qīnrúyìjiā	mother 母亲 mǔqīn father 父亲 fùqīn

verb

noun

Compound element

erect/stand

站

Compound element

 occupy

stand; be on one's feet; stop

station; stop; service

Note in Chinese

站 = +

左边立（P242立）着一个人或物，右边是一个位置，组合后表达人或物立于此地。

🎵 **READ ALOUD**

This flag tells me where I am supposed to STAND. STAND is zhàn（站）.

Stroke order

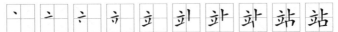

Composite capabilities: 1 2 3 4 5 6 7 8 9 10

prefix/phrase	suffix/phrase
stand 站立 zhànlì	weather station 气象站
platform 站台 zhàntái	qìxiàng zhàn
head of station 站长 zhànzhǎng	station 车站 chēzhàn
	rail station 火车站 huǒchē zhàn
	bus stop 汽车站 qìchē zhàn

Ancient character

noun

verb

Compound element
衤 *clothes*

被

Compound element
皮 *animal fur*

quilt; cover

a passive code

Note in Chinese

被 = 衤 + 皮

左边是衣（P265
衣）服的偏旁 衤，
右边是皮，组合后表
示动物跟人不同，它
们的皮冬天是被子，
夏天是衣服。

READ ALOUD

For a lot of animals, their fur also serves as their special QUILT in the winter. QUILT is bèi（被）.

Stroke order

丶 丷 衤 衤 衤 衤 初 袝 被 被

Composite capabilities: 1 2 3 4 5 6 7 8 9 10

prefix/phrase	suffix/phrase
quilt 被子 bèizi the face of quilt 被面 bèimiàn defendant 被告 bèigào passive 被动 bèidòng a lot of people were bitten 很多人被打了 hěnduō rén bèi dǎ le	cotton quilt 棉被 miánbèi vegetation 植被 zhíbèi

Ancient
character

Compound element
手 hand

verb

看

kàn: *see; read;*
consider; look;
watch; call on;
depend on; mind

kān: *look after;*
keep an eye on

Compound element
目 eyes

Note in Chinese

看 = 手 + 目

上面是手（P222
手），下面是眼
睛。组合后是把手
遮在眼睛上，可以
看得更清楚。

READ ALOUD

Blocking the sun with one hand enables us to SEE better on a bright day.
SEE is kàn（看）.

Stroke order

Composite capabilities: 1 2 3 4 5 6 7 8 9 10

prefix/phrase	suffix/phrase
read book 看书 kànshū	good looking 好看 hǎokàn
go to a hospital 看病 kànbìng	ugly 难看 nánkàn
opinion 看法 kànfǎ	look carefully 看看 kànkan
saw 看见 kànjiàn	
regard as 看作 kànzuò	
look after the house 看家 kānjiā	

Ancient
character

noun
verb
adverb

Compound element
木 *tree*

相

Compound element
目 *eyes*

Note in Chinese

相 = 木 + 目

左边是树木（P192
木），右边是眼睛
（目），组合后显
示古代人生活在
树林里，他们常常
藏在树上，观察地
面。

xiàng: picture; looks;
   appearance

xiāng: see for oneself;
   look at; assist

each other

🦜 READ ALOUD

A small animal keeps watch from within the trunk of a tree, taking a
mental PICTURE of its environment. PICTURE is xiàng（相）.

Stroke order

一	十	才	木	木	机	相	相	相

Composite capabilities: 1 2 3 4 5 6 7 8 9 10

prefix/phrase	suffix/phrase
camera 相机 xiàngjī	take pictures 照相 zhàoxiàng
be in love with each other	facial features 面相 miànxiàng
相爱 xiāng'ài	
compare 相比 xiāngbǐ	
opposite to each other 相对 xiāngduì	
be similar 相像 xiāngxiàng	

Ancient character

noun
measure word

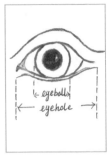

eyeball
eyehole

Compound element
目 *eyes*

眼

Compound element
艮 *something has related to eyes*

eye; look;
a small hole;
key point

Note in Chinese

眼 = 目 + 艮

左边是"目",是
眼睛的总称,右边
的"目+艮"是目中
的球体;在远古,
"目"即是眼睛。
"眼"是眼睛后来
的称谓。

🔊 **READ ALOUD**

An EYE does not float independently. It is firmly set within an eye socket!
EYE is yǎn(眼).

Stroke order

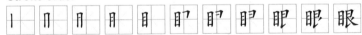

Composite capabilities: 1 2 3 4 5 6 7 8 9 10

prefix/phrase	suffix/phrase
eyes 眼睛 yǎnjing	short-sighted 近视眼 jìnshìyǎn
eyeball 眼球 yǎnqiú	hole 洞眼 dòngyǎn
spectacles 眼镜 yǎnjìng	pinprick 针眼 zhēnyǎn
before one's eye 眼前 yǎnqián	
field of vision 眼界 yǎnjiè	

Ancient
character

Compound element
曰 speak

noun
verb

电

electricity;
telegram; cable

get an electronic
shock

Compound element
∟ wire

Note in Chinese

电 = 曰 + ∟

这是"電"的简体。
这个字由"曰"
（说）与一条竖弯
线组合，表示天气
与地气常以雷电的
方式对话。古体很
像两只大手抓住一
根通天的弯棍。

⚡ **READ ALOUD**

Lightning strikes an open field. ELECTRICITY is the language of Heaven
and Earth. ELECTRICITY is diàn（电）.

Stroke order

丨	冂	冃	曰	电

Composite capabilities: 1 2 3 4 5 6 7 8 9 10

prefix/phrase	suffix/phrase
lamp 电灯 diàndēng	generate electricity 发电 fādiàn
film 电影 diànyǐng	recharge 充电 chōngdiàn
telephone 电话 diànhuà	
broadcasting station 电台 diàntái	
TV 电视 diànshì	
email 电子邮件 diànzǐ yóujiàn	

Ancient character

noun

Compound element

田 *farmland*

Compound element

Note in Chinese

田 = 田

这个字是古代井田
耕作的写照。

farmland;
field; cropland

🌏 **READ ALOUD**

This FARMLAND is divided into four equal parts. FARMLAND is
tián（田）.

Stroke order

Composite capabilities: 1 **2** 3 4 5 6 7 8 9 10

prefix/phrase	suffix/phrase
farmland 田地 tiándì	farming 种田 zhòngtián
landed property 田产 tiánchǎn	rice field 水田 shuǐtián
athletics 田径 tiánjìng	

Ancient character

Compound element

田 farmland

noun

男

man; male; son; boy

baron

Compound element

力 force

Note in Chinese

男 = + ⺁

上面是农田（P250
田），下面是人在
用力（P89力）犁
地。组合后表示古
代男耕女织。

🔊 **READ ALOUD**

MEN used to work the land with simple ploughs. MAN is nán（男）.

Stroke order

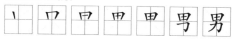

Composite capabilities: 1 2 3 4 5 6 7 8 9 10

prefix/phrase	suffix/phrase
man 男人 nánrén	regard men as superior to women
male 男子 nánzǐ	重男轻女 zhòng nán qīng nǚ
male and female 男女 nánnǚ	
man student 男生 nánshēng	
menswear 男服 nánfú	

Ancient character

Compound element
田 farmland

adjective
verb
noun

累

tired; weary;
fatigued

tire; wear out;
work hard

Compound element
系 silk-tied

Note in Chinese

累 = 田 + 糸

上边是田（P250
田），下面是蚕丝，
组合后表示户外户
内，种田和纺线都
要做。

🕸 **READ ALOUD**

Working in the fields and spinning silk all day is very TIRING! TIRED is
lèi（累）.

Stroke order

Composite capabilities: 1 2 3 4 5 6 7 8 9 10

prefix/phrase	suffix/phrase
hard works 累活儿 lèihuór	tired 劳累 láolèi
tiring 累人 lèirén	fruit hanging heavy on the tree
work oneself to death 累死累活	果实累累 guǒshíléiléi
lèisǐlèihuó	
add up 累计 lěijì	

Ancient character

noun

Compound element
钅（金）*metal*

钱

Compound element

linked materials

currency; copper coin; money; cash; fund

Note in Chinese

钱 = 金 + 戋

这是"錢"的简体。左边是制作金属的作坊（P295金），右边是用绳子串起的货币。

⚜ READ ALOUD

Metal coins were strung together and used as CURRENCY. CURRENCY is qián（钱）.

Stroke order

| 丿 | 𠂉 | 𠂉 | 钅 | 钅 | 钅 | 钅 | 钱 | 钱 | 钱 |

Composite capabilities: 1 2 3 4 5 6 7 8 9 10

prefix/phrase	suffix/phrase
coins 钱币 qiánbì	salary 工钱 gōngqián
wallet 钱包 qiánbāo	be rich 有钱 yǒuqián
wealth 钱财 qiáncái	be poor 没钱 méiqián

Ancient
character

noun
adjective

Compound element
钅 *gold/metal*

银

Compound element
艮 *changes
the meaning
to something
related*

silver; relating to
currency; silver-
coloured

Note in Chinese

银 = 钅 + 艮

金（P295金）与艮
的组合是表达与金
的价值相对的另一
种有价值的金属
"银"。

☉ READ ALOUD

Gold and SILVER are both precious metals but silver is worth less than
gold. SILVER is yín（银）.

Stroke order

| ノ | ト | ヒ | 年 | 钅 | 钅 | 钅 | 钅 | 钼 | 银 |

Composite capabilities: 1 2 3 4 5 6 7 8 9 10

prefix/phrase	suffix/phrase
bank 银行 yínháng	gold silver and treasure 金银财宝
banker 银行家 yínhángjiā	jīnyíncáibǎo
silver medal 银牌 yínpái	

Ancient
character

noun

verb

Compound element
矢 *arrow*

知

Compound element
口 *mouth*

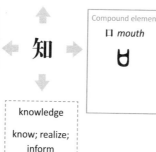

knowledge

know; realize;
inform

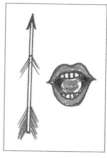

Note in Chinese

知 = 矢 + 口
左边是箭，右文是
说话的口。组合后
表示语言的力量来
自于知识。

⊛ READ ALOUD

KNOWLEDGE regarding the enemy's tactics is best passed on verbally in
battle. KNOWLEDGE is zhī（知）.

Stroke order

Composite capabilities: 1 2 3 4 5 6 7 8 9 10

prefix/phrase	suffix/phrase
knowledge 知识 zhīshi	notify 告知 gàozhī
know 知道 zhīdào	inform 通知 tōngzhī
intellectual 知识分子 zhīshi fènzǐ	ignorant 无知 wúzhī
intimate 知己 zhījǐ	
consciousness 知觉 zhījué	
be content with one's lot 知足 zhīzú	

Ancient character

adjective
verb
noun

Compound element
矢 *arrow*

短

Compound element
豆
food container

short; brief
lack
weak point

Note in Chinese

短 = 矢 + 豆
左边是箭，右文是古代装食品的容器。组合后暗指长度比箭短的东西属于"短"。

· 🔊 READ ALOUD ·

In ancient China, anything measuring under the length of an arrow was classified as SHORT. SHORT is duǎn（短）.

Stroke order

ノ	ト	ᅩ	チ	矢	矢	矢	矢	矩	短

短	短

Composite capabilities: 1 2 3 4 **5** 6 7 8 9 10

prefix/phrase	suffix/phrase
short and small 短小 duǎnxiǎo	length 长短 chángduǎn
short-distance run 短跑 duǎnpǎo	

Ancient
character

noun

Compound element
禾 *crops*

Compound element
火 *flam*

autumn; fall;
harvest time;
year; a period
time

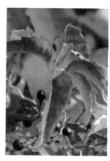

Note in Chinese

秋 = 禾 + 火

左边是一株成熟的
谷穗，右文是火
（P180火）苗。组
合后是显示谷子收
获，一片火红，是
秋实的季节。

READ ALOUD

Leaves turn a beautiful flame-red in the AUTUMN. AUTUMN is
qiū（秋）.

Stroke order

Composite capabilities: 1 2 3 4 5 6 7 8 9 10

prefix/phrase	suffix/phrase
autumn 秋天 qiūtiān	The beginning of autumn 立秋 lìqiū
the season of autumn 秋季 qiūjì	wonderful autumn 金秋 jīnqiū
autumn wind 秋风 qiūfēng	
swing(for play) 秋千 qiūqiān	

Ancient character

Compound element

ripe crops/ cooked crops

noun adjective

香

fragrant; sweet-smelling; delicious; savoury; sound

perfume; joss stick

Compound element

mouth

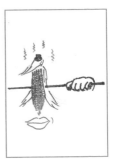

Note in Chinese

香 = 禾 + ﹒﹕+ 口
上面是成熟后的农作物和它们散出的气味。下面是张开的口。

⊙ **READ ALOUD**

The FRAGRANCE of freshly roasted corn is irresistible! FRAGRANT is xiāng（香）.

Stroke order

Composite capabilities: 1 2 3 4 5 6 7 8 9 10

prefix/phrase	suffix/phrase
fragrance 香味 xiāngwèi	burn joss sticks 烧香 shāoxiāng
a sweet smell 香气 xiāngqì	be very popular 吃香 chīxiāng
perfume 香水 xiāngshuǐ	
sausage 香肠 xiāngcháng	
banana 香蕉 xiāngjiāo	

Ancient character

noun
verb
measure word

Compound element
禾 *crops*

Compound element
中 *centre*

Note in Chinese

种 = 禾 + 中

这是"種"的简体。左边是作物的秧苗，右文是表示位置的"中"（P17 中），组合后表明下种时，种子要放在正中。

zhǒng: seed; species; race

zhòng: plant; grow; cultivate

kind; sort

🔊 READ ALOUD

For a seed to grow well, it is best to PLANT it in the middle of the pot. PLANT is zhòng（种）.

Stroke order

Composite capabilities: 1 2 **3** 4 5 6 7 8 9 10

prefix/phrase	suffix/phrase
cultivate land 种地 zhòngdì	breeding 育种 yùzhǒng
grow flowers 种花 zhònghuā	
seed 种子 zhǒngzi	
race 种族 zhǒngzú	

Ancient character

Compound element 𠂆 vine

noun

瓜

melon; gourd

Note in Chinese

瓜 = 𠂆 + 厶

这是一个象形字。

Compound element 厶 round-shaped-fruit

🔊 READ ALOUD

This character looks like a single MELON hanging on a bamboo frame.
MELON is guā（瓜）.

Stroke order

一 厂 厂 瓜 瓜

Composite capabilities: 1 2 3 4 5 6 7 8 9 10

prefix/phrase	suffix/phrase
melons and fruits 瓜果 guāguǒ	watermelon 西瓜 xīguā
melon seeds 瓜子 guāzǐ	pumpkin 南瓜 nánguā
divide up 瓜分 guāfēn	fool 傻瓜 shǎguā

Ancient character

Compound element
鸟 bird

noun   *bird*

鸟

Note in Chinese

鸟 =

这是"鸟"的简体。上面的一点是鸟的顶翅，中间一点代表它的眼睛。

Compound element

READ ALOUD

This BIRD has a beautiful punk hairstyle! BIRD is niǎo（鸟）.

Stroke order

Composite capabilities: 1 2 3 4 5 6 7 8 9 10

prefix/phrase	suffix/phrase
small bird 鸟儿 niǎor	small bird 小鸟 xiǎoniǎo
birds 鸟类 niǎolèi	woodpecker 啄木鸟 zhuómùniǎo
on a fine spring day 鸟语花香 niǎoyǔhuāxiāng	

Ancient character

Compound element

穴 cave

adjective
noun
adverb
verb

空

kōng: *empty; hollow*

sky; air

for nothing; in vain

kòng: *leave empty*

Compound element

工 work

工

Note in Chinese

空 = 穴 + 工

上面是一个石洞，
下面是一个工事。

🐾 READ ALOUD

This cave is not EMPTY, it houses a work of beautiful craftsmanship.
EMPTY is kōng（空）.

Stroke order

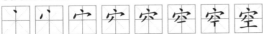

Composite capabilities: 1 2 3 4 5 6 7 8 9 10

prefix/phrase	suffix/phrase
air 空气 kōngqì	in the sky 上空 shàngkōng
space 空间 kōngjiān	be free 得空 dékòng
daydream 空想 kōngxiǎng	busy 没空 méikòng
in the sky 空中 kōngzhōng	
air disaster 空难 kōngnàn	

Ancient character

Compound element

穴 cave

adverb
verb

突

suddenly;
abruptly;
unexpectedly

dash forward;
charge into;
sticking out

Compound element

犬 dog

Note in Chinese

突 = 穴 + 犬

上面是一个石洞，下面是一只狗。组合后表示一条狗从石洞里冲出来。

⚘ READ ALOUD

This dog leapt out of the cave SUDDENLY, giving everyone a fright. SUDDENLY is tū（突）.

Stroke order

Composite capabilities: 1 2 3 4 5 6 7 8 9 10

prefix/phrase	suffix/phrase
suddenly 突然 tūrán	conflict 冲突 chōngtū
attack without warning 突击 tūjī	
suddenly occur 突发 tūfā	

Ancient character

Compound element
穴 cave

verb
noun

容

accommodate;
hold; contain;
tolerate; permit;
allow

facial expression;
appearance;
looks

Compound element

人 + 口（谷）
population

Note in Chinese

容 = 宀 + 人 + 口

上面是石洞，下面
是人们张开的口。
组合后表示洞穴的
空间可供人们生
活、居住。

🕮 READ ALOUD

Caves have been useful ACCOMMODATION throughout history.
ACCOMMODATE is róng（容）.

Stroke order

Composite capabilities: 1 2 3 4 5 6 7 8 9 10

prefix/phrase	suffix/phrase
take shelter 容身 róngshēn	face 面容 miànróng
tolerate 容忍 róngrěn	describe 形容 xíngróng
regard people with kindly tolerance	content 内容 nèiróng
容人 róngrén	
easy 容易 róngyì	

Ancient character

Compound element

衣 clothes

noun

clothes

Note in Chinese

衣 =

这个字是一套古代的衣帽挂在一起的样子。

Compound element

🔧 READ ALOUD

It is best to hang up your CLOTHES after use if you don't like ironing! CLOTHES is yī（衣）.

Stroke order

Composite capabilities: 1 2 3 4 5 6 7 8 9 10

prefix/phrase	suffix/phrase
clothes 衣服 yīfu	underwear 内衣 nèiyī
coat hanger 衣架 yījià	jacket 外衣 wàiyī
wardrobe 衣柜 yīguì	overcoat 大衣 dàyī
	raincoat 雨衣 yǔyī
	windcheater 风衣 fēngyī

Ancient character

Compound element
亠 + 毛
a hat and hair

noun
verb

表

appearance;
outside; surface

show; express

Compound element
衣 outfit

Note in Chinese

表 = 𠔼 + 𧘇

上面是帽子，中间
是毛发，下面是大
衣（P265衣）。组
合后显示衣冠整洁
的外表。

🔊 **READ ALOUD**

A person's APPEARANCE often reflects his inner life. APPEARANCE is
biǎo（表）.

Stroke order

Composite capabilities: 1 2 3 4 5 6 7 8 9 10

prefix/phrase	suffix/phrase
express 表达 biǎodá	appearance 外表 wàibiǎo
display 表现 biǎoxiàn	publish 发表 fābiǎo
surface 表面 biǎomiàn	

Ancient
character

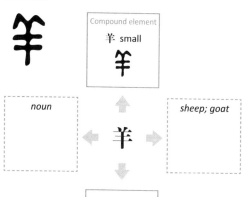

| | Compound element |
| | 羊 small |

noun   羊   *sheep; goat*

Compound element

Note in Chinese

羊 = 羊
上面是两只角，下
面是头。

🎵 READ ALOUD

This character looks like the head of a proud RAM. RAM is yáng（羊）.

Stroke order

Composite capabilities: 1 2 3 4 5 6 7 8 9 10

prefix/phrase	suffix/phrase
mutton 羊肉 yángròu	sheep 绵羊 miányáng
lamb 羊羔 yánggāo	goat 山羊 shānyáng
sheep milk 羊奶 yángnǎi	
wool 羊毛 yángmáo	

Ancient character

Compound element

羊（羊）

sheep

adjective
verb
noun

美

delicious; good;
beautiful; very
satisfactory

beautify; be
pleased with
oneself

Compound element

大 big/most

Note in Chinese

美 = 羊 + 大

羊（P267羊）在
上面，下面是一个
"大"（P123大），
组合后表达羊在古
代家畜里的地位很
高。

⚙ READ ALOUD

Of all meats, mutton is considered by many to be the most DELICIOUS.
DELICIOUS is měi（美）.

Stroke order

Composite capabilities: 1 2 3 4 5 6 7 8 9 10

prefix/phrase	suffix/phrase
delicious food 美味 měiwèi	praise 赞美 zànměi
good wine 美酒 měijiǔ	beauty contest 选美 xuǎnměi
make up 美容 měiróng	love to be beautiful 爱美 àiměi
the United States(U.S.A) 美国 Měiguó	
U.S. dollar 美元 měiyuán	

Ancient
character

Compound element

—

the ear of grain

noun
measure word

米

rice

metre

Note in Chinese

米 = ⺊ + ⺊⺊

这个字是象形字，
有谷穗和谷粒。

Compound element

 rices

---

🔊 READ ALOUD

The Union Jack looks just like the Chinese character for RICE. RICE is
mǐ（米）.

Stroke order

Composite capabilities: 1 2 3 4 5 6 7 8 9 10

prefix/phrase	suffix/phrase
cooked rice 米饭 mǐfàn	rice 大米 dàmǐ
cream-coloured 米色 mǐsè	corn 玉米 yùmǐ
Mickey Mouse 米老鼠 Mǐlǎoshǔ	two metres tall
	两米高 liǎng mǐ gāo

Ancient character

Compound element
old full-bearded person

verb

考

test; exam; check; inspect; study; investigate

Compound element
ʒ walking stick

Note in Chinese

考 = 丬 + ʒ

上面是一个长发的人，长长的一撇是胡须，下面是协助行走的木棍。

🔊 READ ALOUD

This bearded old man has to pass his TEST before driving a wheelchair! TEST is kǎo（考）.

Stroke order

Composite capabilities: 1 2 3 4 5 6 7 8 9 10

prefix/phrase	suffix/phrase
examination questions 考题 kǎotí	final exam 大考 dàkǎo
exam 考试 kǎoshì	driving test 路考 lùkǎo
archaeology 考古 kǎogǔ	

Ancient character

Compound element

 old full-bearded person

adjective	老	old; experienced; tough
noun		old people
verb		overgrown
adverb		for a long time; very; always

Compound element

匕tool

Note in Chinese

老 =  + 

上面是一个长发的人，长长的一撇是胡须，下面是协助行走的木棍。

READ ALOUD

A very OLD man usually requires either a stick or a wheelchair to get around. OLD is lǎo（老）.

Stroke order

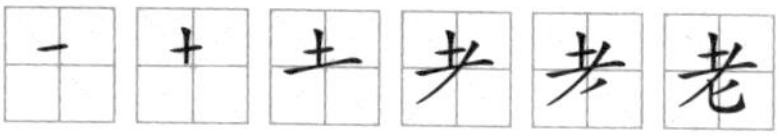

Composite capabilities: 1 2 3 4 5 6 7 8 9 10

prefix/phrase	suffix/phrase
old people 老人 lǎorén	aged 年老 niánlǎo
teacher 老师 lǎoshī	pension 养老金 yǎnglǎojīn
Old Li 老李 Lǎo Lǐ	flaunt one's seniority 倚老卖老 yǐlǎomàilǎo
honestly 老实 lǎoshi	
always 老是 lǎoshì	

Ancient character

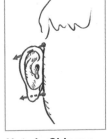

noun

Compound element

耳 *ear*

耳

Compound element

ear

Note in Chinese

耳 =

这是一只右耳的象
形字。

🔊 **READ ALOUD**

Some people like to have piercings in their EARS, one at the top, one at the bottom. EAR is ěr（耳）.

Stroke order

Composite capabilities: 1 2 3 4 5 6 7 8 9 10

prefix/phrase	suffix/phrase
ear 耳朵 ěrduo	
earrings 耳环 ěrhuán	
earphone 耳机 ěrjī	

Ancient
character

Compound element

页 page

noun

页

page

Note in Chinese

页 = 頁

这 是 " 页 " 的 简
体，是一个大头的
人。本字与"首"
同字，"页"后来
生成了新义。

Compound element

🔊 READ ALOUD

It takes a good head to master all the PAGES of all the books at college!
PAGE is yè（页）.

Stroke order

Composite capabilities: 1 2 3 4 5 6 7 8 9 10

prefix/phrase	suffix/phrase
the total number of page	the first page 首页 shǒuyè
页数 yèshù	insert page 插页 chāyè
the page 页面 yèmiàn	the first ten pages
number of page 页码 yèmǎ	前十页 qiánshíyè

Ancient character

noun
verb

| Compound element
彡 *beard*
 | 须 | Compound element
页 *head*
 |

beard;
moustache

must; have to

Note in Chinese

须 = 彡 +

这是"鬚"的简
体。左边是三绺长
须，右边是一个人
头（P273页），组
合后表示胡须。

🔊 **READ ALOUD**

A man with a lot of facial HAIR has to groom it regularly or it will reach the floor in no time! HAIR is xū（须）.

Stroke order

Composite capabilities: 1 2 3 4 5 6 7 8 9 10

prefix/phrase	suffix/phrase
beard and hair 须发 xūfà	must 必须 bìxū
it must be understood	
须知 xūzhī	
feeler 须子 xūzi	

Ancient
character

noun
verb

Compound element
是 *to be*

题

Compound element
页 *head/ page*

Note in Chinese

题 = 昰 + 頁

左上是太阳，左下
是脚走的路；合起
来是"是"（P211
是），右文是脑子
"页"（P273页），
组合后表示有一个
题目需要思索。

subject; topic;
title

inscribe

READ ALOUD

'To be or not to be' is a tricky SUBJECT that requires a good head to
ponder. SUBJECT is tí（题）.

Stroke order

| 丨 | 冂 | 日 | 日 | 旦 | 早 | 早 | 昰 | 是 | 是 |

| 是 | 是 | 题 | 题 | 题 |

Composite capabilities: 1 2 3 4 5 6 7 8 9 10

prefix/phrase	suffix/phrase
subject 题目 tímù	question 问题 wèntí
explanatory notes on the topic	main topic 主题 zhǔtí
题解 tíjiě	assign a topic 命题 mìngtí
write a few words of commemoration	
题字 tízì	
digression 题外话 tíwàihuà	

Ancient
character

adjective

Compound element
舌 *tongue*

甜

Compound element
廿 *sweetly*

sweet; sound

Note in Chinese

甜 = 舌 + 甘

今字与古体左右部件
相反。今体左上是
"千"，"很多"之
意，左下是口舌；右
边是一个容器，里
面一横表示甜，组
合后表达知甜是舌
头味觉功能之一。

- ✿ **READ ALOUD** -

The tongue loves the taste of SWEETNESS. SWEET is tián（甜）.

Stroke order

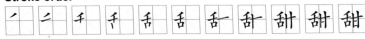

Composite capabilities: 1 2 3 4 5 6 7 8 9 10

prefix/phrase	suffix/phrase
sweet food 甜食 tiánshí	fragrant and sweet 香甜 xiāngtián
muskmelon 甜瓜 tiánguā	
beet 甜菜 tiáncài	
sweet 甜美 tiánměi	

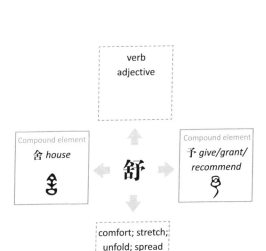

verb
adjective

Compound element
舍 *house*

舒

Compound element
予 *give/grant/ recommend*

comfort; stretch; unfold; spread

leisurely

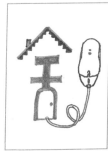

Note in Chinese

舒 = 舍 + 予

左上是屋顶，左下是墙壁与窗子；右边是"助"，组合后表达延伸。

🎵 READ ALOUD

It is good manners to offer guests the most COMFORTABLE room in the house. COMFORT is shū（舒）.

Stroke order

| ノ | ﾉ | ﾄ | ﾄ | 亼 | 牟 | 舎 | 舍 | 舍 | 舒 |

| 舒 | 舒 |

Composite capabilities: 1 2 3 4 5 6 7 8 9 10

prefix/phrase	suffix/phrase
comfortable 舒服 shūfu	
unfold 舒展 shūzhǎn	
happy 舒心 shūxīn	

Ancient character

Compound element

⺮ (竹)
bamboo/eyes
⺮

verb
adverb

算

count; calculate;
reckon; include;
plan; guess;
consider
at long last;
in the end

Note in Chinese

算 = ⺮ + 具

上面是眼睛，中间
是算盘，下面是手
指。

Compound element

 hands on
the abacus

🍀 **READ ALOUD**

When COUNTING sums, we need to focus with both our eyes and our fingers. COUNT is suàn（算）.

Stroke order

| ノ | ⼃ | ⺺ | ⺮ | 竹 | ⺮ | 竹 | 筲 | 筲 | 笡 |

| 筲 | 筲 | 算 | 算 |

Composite capabilities: 1 2 3 4 5 6 7 8 9 10

prefix/phrase	suffix/phrase
mathematics 算术 suànshù	plan 打算 dǎsuàn
the way of calculate 算法 suànfǎ	calculator 计算机 jìsuànjī
fortune telling 算命 suànmìng	worthwhile 上算 shàngsuàn

Ancient character

Compound element

自 self

pronoun
adverb
conjunction

自

self; oneself; one's own

certainly; of course

from; since

Compound element

Note in Chinese

自 = 𦣻

上面的一撇是指示符，代表手指；下面的"目"不是眼睛而是鼻子的象形。组合后表示用手指鼻子，即"自己"。

🎵 **READ ALOUD**

My nose is a representation of my SELF. SELF is zì（自）.

Stroke order

Composite capabilities: 1 2 3 4 5 6 7 8 9 **10**

prefix/phrase	suffix/phrase
oneself 自己 zìjǐ	personally 亲自 qīnzì
self-respect 自爱 zì'ài	alone 独自 dúzì
support oneself 自立 zìlì	privately 私自 sīzì
self-important 自大 zìdà	
act on one's own 自主 zìzhǔ	
since 自从 zìcóng	

Ancient character

noun

Compound element
舟 *boat*

船

Compound element
台
few people

boat; ship

Note in Chinese

船 = 月 + 台

左边是一只小船，
右上表示数字，右下
是代表人的"口"。
组合后显示是水上
的住所。

READ ALOUD

Quite a few people live on this tiny BOAT. BOAT is chuán（船）.

Stroke order

Composite capabilities: 1 2 3 4 5 6 7 8 9 10

prefix/phrase	suffix/phrase
captain 船长 chuánzhǎng	steamboat 汽船 qìchuán
the body of a ship 船体 chuántǐ	space craft 太空船 tàikōngchuán
shipment 船运 chuányùn	
the owner of a ship 船主 chuánzhǔ	

Ancient character

Compound element

大 hand

verb
noun

系

tie; bind; fasten;
to be

system;
department

Note in Chinese

系 = 大 + 糸

这是"繫"的简体。上面是拴住的绳子，中间是两个蚕茧，下面是手。

Compound element

糸 silk cocoons

READ ALOUD

Silk threads are often used to TIE together hanging lanterns. TIE is
xì（系）.

Stroke order

Composite capabilities: 1 2 3 4 5 6 7 8 9 10

prefix/phrase	suffix/phrase
series 系列 xìliè	contact 联系 liánxì
TV soap 系列剧 xìlièjù	relation 关系 guānxì
head of department of university	system 体系 tǐxì
系主任 xì zhǔrèn	department of literature 文学系
	wénxuéxì

Ancient character

Compound element

土 (大)
earth
(big)

verb

走

walk; go; run; move; leave; visit; through; escape; depart from...

Note in Chinese

走 = 土 (大) + 止
上面是甩开的双臂，下面是迈开的大步。

Compound element

止 foot/stop
止

🔊 READ ALOUD

WALKING is still the main means of travel in the countryside. WALK is zǒu（走）.

Stroke order

Composite capabilities: 1 2 3 4 5 6 7 8 9 10

prefix/phrase	suffix/phrase
go on foot 走路 zǒulù	move fast 快步走 kuàibùzǒu
have good luck 走运 zǒuyùn	stroll around 走走 zǒuzǒu
pavement 走道 zǒudào	
leave a work 走人 zǒurén	

Ancient character

verb
measure word

Compound element
走 *walking*

起

Compound element
己 *self*

Note in Chinese

起 = 走 + 己

左边是走（P282
走），右边是自己
（P161己）。

rise; get up;
remove; appear;
grow; build;
set up; start; up

instance

🔊 READ ALOUD

A child would fall and RAISE himself up many times before he learns to walk. RISE is qǐ（起）.

Stroke order

Composite capabilities: 1 2 3 4 5 6 7 8 9 **10**

prefix/phrase	suffix/phrase
start 起动 qǐdòng	get together 一起 yìqǐ
starting point 起点 qǐdiǎn	get up late from bed 晚起 wǎnqǐ
catch fire 起火 qǐhuǒ	look down 看不起 kànbuqǐ
stand up 起立 qǐlì	
sue 起诉 qǐsù	

Ancient
character

verb

Compound element
走 *road/walk*

超

Compound element
召 *flourishing*

surpass;
exceed; take
a short cut

Note in Chinese

超 = 走 + 召

左边是迈开步子走
（P282走），右上
是举起的手，右下
是叫喊着的口，组
合后表示从脚力到
精神都强于他人。

🔊 READ ALOUD

The athlete greets the cheering crowds. He has SURPASSED his own
record! SURPASS is chāo（超）.

Stroke order

Composite capabilities: 1 2 3 4 5 6 7 8 9 10

prefix/phrase	suffix/phrase
surpass 超过 chāoguò	super 高超 gāochāo
ahead of times 超前 chāoqián	catch up with and surpass 赶超
supermarket 超市 chāoshì	gǎnchāo

Ancient
character

Compound element

田 farmland

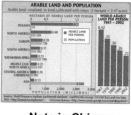

*noun
measure word
preposition
adverb*

里

*home; lining;
inside; inner;
neighbourhood;
native place*

mile

in; inside

Compound element

土 soil

Note in Chinese

里 = 田 + 土

上面是一块耕田
（P250田），下面是
土（P120土）地。组
合后表示可耕之地
是人们创建邻里家
乡的处所。

🔊 **READ ALOUD**

Homes and NEIGHBOURHOODS are often built near arable land.
NEIGHBOURHOOD is lǐ（里）.

Stroke order

Composite capabilities: 1 2 **3** 4 5 6 7 8 9 10

prefix/phrase	suffix/phrase
inside 里边 lǐbian	hometown 故里 gùlǐ
inside 里头 lǐtou	home village 乡里 xiānglǐ
inside and outside 里外 lǐwài	kilometre 公里 gōnglǐ

Ancient character

Compound element
口
kneecap/mouth

noun
adjective
adverb

足

foot

enough;
sufficient

fully; as much as

Compound element
止 leg/foot

Note in Chinese

足 = 口 + 止

口在上，是膝盖；
下面是小腿和脚。

READ ALOUD

Words are not enough, we also need action! The mouth and the FEET are good partners in life. FOOT is zú（足）.

Stroke order

Composite capabilities: 1 **2** 3 4 5 6 7 8 9 10

prefix/phrase	suffix/phrase
enough 足够 zúgòu	be content with reasonable level
football 足球 zúqiú	知足 zhīzú
sufficiently 足以 zúyǐ	flatfoot 平足 píngzú

verb

Compound element

趼 (足) foot

跑

Compound element

包 *energy is hiding inside the container*

Note in Chinese

跑 = 趼 + 包

左边是腿脚（P286 足），右文是表示里面有能量的"包"（P77包）。

run; run a race; run about doing something; away

🔊 READ ALOUD

To RUN fast, our legs have to be propelled by a massive amount of energy. RUN is pǎo（跑）.

Stroke order

Composite capabilities: 1 2 3 4 5 6 7 8 9 10

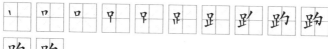

prefix/phrase	suffix/phrase
run 跑步 pǎobù	long-distance running
runway 跑道 pǎodào	长跑 chángpǎo
track shoes 跑鞋 pǎoxié	short-distance running
	短跑 duǎnpǎo

Ancient
character

noun
verb
preposition
conjunction

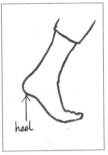

heel

Note in Chinese

跟 =

左边是腿脚，右边
是"艮"。"艮"
的加入表达了与偏
旁原义（整个的
足）相对的足跟部
位"跟"。

Compound element
⻊（足）foot

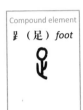

跟

Compound element

艮 *changes
the meaning
to something
related*

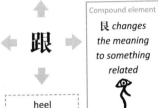

heel
to follow
towards;
and

READ ALOUD

To follow somebody we need both our toes and our HEELS! HEEL is
gēn（跟）.

Stroke order

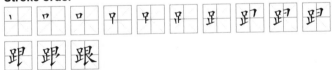

Composite capabilities: 1 2 3 4 5 6 7 8 9 10

prefix/phrase	suffix/phrase
catch up with 跟上 gēnshàng	you and me 你跟我 nǐ gēn wǒ
follow 跟从 gēncóng	heel 脚跟 jiǎogēn
	follow up 紧跟 jǐngēn

Ancient
character

noun

Compound element

足（足）*foot*

路

各

*each/
individual*

way; road; path;
journey; line;
region; route;
sort; grade

Note in Chinese

路 = 足 + 各

左边是腿脚，右上
是脚印，右下是城
门的出口，组合后
表示每个人有自己
的路。

⏺ **READ ALOUD**

Once past the city gates, everyone goes their separate WAY. WAY is
lù（路）.

Stroke order

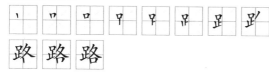

Composite capabilities: 1 2 3 **4** 5 6 7 8 9 10

prefix/phrase	suffix/phrase
journey 路程 lùchéng	road 道路 dàolù
street lamp 路灯 lùdēng	public road 公路 gōnglù
passerby 路人 lùrén	way of thinking 思路 sīlù
crossing 路口 lùkǒu	have good connection with 有路子 yǒu lùzi

Ancient character

verb

Compound element
⻊（足）foot

踢

Compound element

exchange/
raise/ upward

Note in Chinese

踢 = ⻊ + 昜

左边是腿脚，右上
是球，右下是扬起
的动作，组合后表
示用脚触球。

kick; play

⚙ READ ALOUD

To KICK a ball into goal, it is necessary to possess both strength and accuracy. KICK is tī（踢）.

Stroke order

| 丶 | 口 | 口 | 甲 | 甲 | 呈 | 足 | 䟡 | 跎 | 跗 |

| 趵 | 跙 | 踢 | 踢 | 踢 |

Composite capabilities: **1** 2 3 4 5 6 7 8 9 10

prefix/phrase	suffix/phrase
play football 踢足球 tī zúqiú	cuff and kick 拳打脚踢
kick the door open 踢开门	quándǎjiǎotī
tīkāi mén	

Ancient character

Compound element
身 body

*noun
measure word*

身

*body;
oneself;
life*

Compound element

Note in Chinese

身 =

这是一个戴着帽子
的人在走路时身体
笔直的样子。

☀ READ ALOUD ·

An English gentleman tends to walk with his BODY upright. BODY is
shēn（身）.

Stroke order

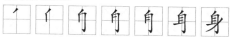

Composite capabilities: 1 2 3 4 5 **6** 7 8 9 10

prefix/phrase	suffix/phrase
body 身体 shēntǐ	family background 出身 chūshēn
height 身高 shēngāo	warm-up 热身 rèshēn
body and mind 身心 shēnxīn	oneself 自身 zìshēn
at one's side 身边 shēnbiān	

Ancient character

Compound element

人

top of horn

noun
measure word

角

horn; bugle;
corner; angle

jiao, fractional
unit of money in
China

Note in Chinese

角 = 人 + 𧢲

上面的是尖形，下面的是角质的骨头。

Compound element

用 horn

𧢲

🔊 **READ ALOUD**

Sharp HORNS make good tools. HORN is jiǎo（角）.

Stroke order

Composite capabilities: 1 2 3 4 5 6 7 8 9 10

prefix/phrase	suffix/phrase
angle 角度 jiǎodù	horn 牛角 niújiǎo
corner 角落 jiǎoluò	corner of room 房角 fángjiǎo
corner(kick) 角球 jiǎoqiú	five-pointed start 五角星 wǔjiǎoxīng

Ancient character

verb
noun

Compound element

角 horn

解

Compound element

axe+ox

dissect;
separate; untie;
dispel; explain;
comprehend

solution

Note in Chinese

解 = 角 + 厶 + 屮

左边是一只牛角
（P292角），右上
是一把斧头，右下
是牛（P221牛）头，
组合后表示牛正在
被肢解。

🎙 **READ ALOUD**

People often DISSECTED oxen to get at their precious horns. DISSECT is jiě（解）.

Stroke order

Composite capabilities: 1 2 3 4 5 6 7 8 9 10

prefix/phrase	suffix/phrase
dissect 解剖 jiěpōu	understand 理解 lǐjiě
answer 解答 jiědá	do not understand 不解 bùjiě
liberate 解放 jiěfàng	ask for solution 求解 qiújiě
disintegrated 解体 jiětǐ	graph 图解 tújiě

Ancient character

verb
noun

Compound element

亻（人）
person

像

Compound element

象 *elephant*

be like; look as if;
such as

likeness; portrait;
image; picture

Note in Chinese

像 = 亻 + 象

左边是一个人，右
文是一堆暴露于地
面的大象的遗骨，
组合后表示古人在
未见到象以前，先
是通过这些遗骨推
想出象的样子。

🐾 **READ ALOUD**

Using the skeletal remains of an elephant, pre-historic man managed to construct an IMAGE of the live animal. IMAGE is xiàng（像）.

Stroke order

Composite capabilities: 1 2 3 4 5 6 7 8 9 10

prefix/phrase	suffix/phrase
reasonable 像话 xiànghuà	be alike 很像 hěn xiàng
up to the mark	drawing 画像 huàxiàng
像模像样 xiàngmúxiàngyàng	portrait 人像 rénxiàng

Ancient character

Compound element

people's mouth

noun adjective

金

gold; metal; money

golden; precious

Note in Chinese

金 = ∧ + ± + ∴

上面是有人在叫，
下面是含有金沙的
矿土。

Compound element

earth + goldmine

🏅 READ ALOUD

When GOLD dust was discovered underground, mining the precious metal became a serious pursuit. GOLD is jīn（金）.

Stroke order

Composite capabilities: 1 2 3 4 5 6 7 8 9 10

prefix/phrase	suffix/phrase
gold 金子 jīnzi	cash 现金 xiànjīn
pyramid 金字塔 jīnzìtǎ	platinum 白金 báijīn
goldmine 金矿 jīnkuàng	
gold medal 金牌 jīnpái	

Ancient character

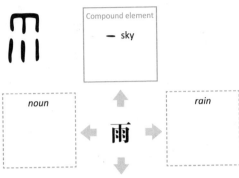

Compound element

— sky

noun

雨

rain

Compound element

ⵏⵏ raindrops

Note in Chinese

雨 = 一 + ⵏⵏ

上面一横是天，下面是雨点（可能是从屋里窗子向外看的雨点）。

⚙ READ ALOUD

Water falling from the sky is called RAIN. RAIN is yǔ（雨）.

Stroke order

Composite capabilities: 1 2 3 4 5 6 7 8 9 10

prefix/phrase	suffix/phrase
rain day 雨天 yǔtiān	drizzle 小雨 xiǎoyǔ
raindrops 雨点 yǔdiǎn	heavy rain 大雨 dàyǔ
umbrella 雨伞 yǔsǎn	rainstorm 暴雨 bàoyǔ
raincoat 雨衣 yǔyī	
galoshes 雨鞋 yǔxié	

Ancient character

noun

Compound element
鱼 *hand*

鱼

Compound element

fish

Note in Chinese

鱼 =

这 是 " 鱼 " 的 简
体。

⚹ **READ ALOUD**

This character looks just like a FISH on a chopping board. FISH is
yú（鱼）.

Stroke order

Composite capabilities: 1 2 3 4 5 6 7 8 9 10

prefix/phrase	suffix/phrase
fishes 鱼类 yúlèi	goldfish 金鱼 jīnyú
the fresh of fish 鱼肉 yúròu	whale 鲸鱼 jīngyú
fish soup 鱼汤 yútāng	mermaid 美人鱼 měirényú

Ancient character

adjective
noun

Compound element
鱼 *fish*

鲜

Compound element
羊 *lamb*

xiān: fresh;
bright-coloured;
delicious; tasty
delicacy; seafood

xiǎn: rare

Note in Chinese

鲜 = 魚 + 羊

这是"鲜"的简
体。左边是一条鱼
（P297鱼），右边
是一头羊（P267
羊）。古人盛宴，
有鱼又有羊，既营
养又鲜美。

⚙ READ ALOUD

Whether ordering fish or mutton in a restaurant, we would expect it to be FRESH! FRESH is xiān（鲜）.

Stroke order

Composite capabilities: 1 2 3 4 5 6 7 8 9 10

prefix/phrase	suffix/phrase
delicious 鲜美 xiānměi	fresh 新鲜 xīnxiān
fresh flowers 鲜花 xiānhuā	
distinctive 鲜明 xiānmíng	
rarely have 鲜有 xiǎnyǒu	

noun

Compound element
革 *leather/ skins of ox*

Compound element
圭 *sharp-shape-stone*

shoes

Note in Chinese

鞋 = 革 + 圭

"鞋" 这个字左边
是 "革"，牛皮，
右边是 "圭"，一
种尖型的小石头；
合在一起表示把皮
革垫在脚下是鞋的
主要功能。

🍀 READ ALOUD

SHOES in the olden days had leather soles for negotiating uneven stone paths. SHOE is xié（鞋）.

Stroke order

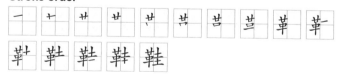

一　十　十　廿　廿　苦　苦　苦　革　革

革†　革†　革†　革†　鞋

Composite capabilities: 1 2 3 4 5 6 7 8 9 10

prefix/phrase	suffix/phrase
shoemaker 鞋匠 xiéjiàng	leather shoes 皮鞋 píxié
shoe shop 鞋店 xiédiàn	trainer 运动鞋 yùndòngxié
sole 鞋底 xiédǐ	high-heel shoes 高跟鞋 gāogēnxié
	skates 冰鞋 bīngxié

Ancient character

Compound element

∧ lid/handle

noun
verb

食

food

eat

Compound element

♀ + 一
food + stand

Note in Chinese

食 = ∧ + ♀ + 一

上面是盖子和提
手，下面是饭菜与
容器的底部，组合
后表示是饭食。

🍂 READ ALOUD

Two-tier containers were used to carry FOOD to workers in the fields.
FOOD is shí（食）.

Stroke order

Composite capabilities: 1 2 3 4 5 6 **7** 8 9 10

prefix/phrase	suffix/phrase
food product 食品 shípǐn	cooked wheaten food 面食 miànshí
used for food 食用 shíyòng	sweets 甜食 tiánshí
break one's promise 食言 shíyán	eatable 可食 kěshí
	solar eclipse 日食 rìshí

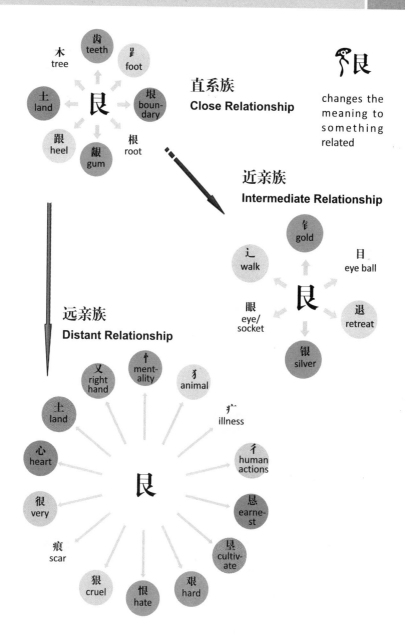

木 tree

齿 teeth

𧾷 foot

土 land

艮

垠 boundary

跟 heel

龈 gum

根 root

艮

changes the meaning to something related

直系族
Close Relationship

近亲族
Intermediate Relationship

钅 gold

辶 walk

目 eye ball

艮

眼 eye/socket

退 retreat

银 silver

远亲族
Distant Relationship

又 right hand

忄 mentality

犭 animal

土 land

疒 illness

心 heart

彳 human actions

很 very

艮

恳 earnest

痕 scar

垦 cultivate

狠 cruel

恨 hate

艰 hard

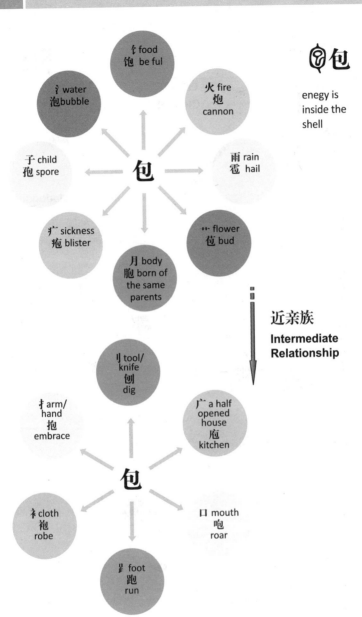

包

enegy is inside the shell

饣 food
饱 be ful

氵 water
泡 bubble

火 fire
炮 cannon

子 child
孢 spore

雨 rain
雹 hail

疒 sickness
疱 blister

艹 flower
苞 bud

月 body
胞 born of the same parents

包

近亲族
Intermediate Relationship

刂 tool/knife
刨 dig

扌 arm/hand
抱 embrace

广 a half opened house
庖 kitchen

衤 cloth
袍 robe

口 mouth
咆 roar

包

𧾷 foot
跑 run

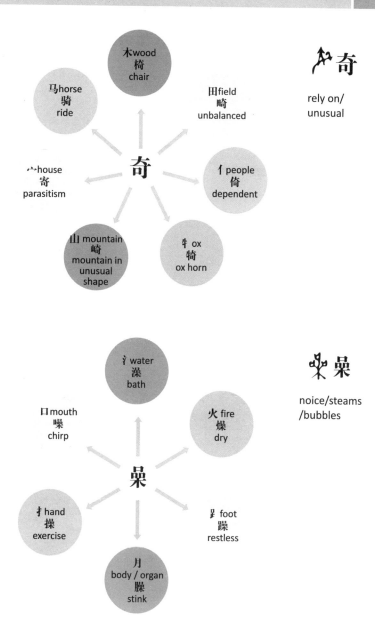

木 wood
椅
chair

马 horse
骑
ride

田 field
畸
unbalanced

宀 house
寄
parasitism

奇

rely on/
unusual

亻 people
倚
dependent

山 mountain
崎
mountain in
unusual
shape

牛 ox
犄
ox horn

氵 water
澡
bath

口 mouth
噪
chirp

火 fire
燥
dry

㬟

noice/steams
/bubbles

扌 hand
操
exercise

足 foot
躁
restless

月
body / organ
臊
stink

Index of Radicals & Characters

	5	民	mín	27
	6	买	mǎi	28
Two strokes				
亠	8	京	jīng	29
	10	高	gāo	30
	10	离	lí	31
冫	6	冰	bīng	32
讠	5	记	jì	33
	5	议	yì	34
	7	识	shí	35
	7	诉	sù	36
	8	话	huà	37
	9	说	shuō	38
	9	语	yǔ	39
	10	读	dú	40
	10	请	qǐng	41
	12	谢	xiè	42
十	8	卖	mài	43
	9	南	nán	44
厂	4	历	lì	45
匚	7	医	yī	46
刂	8	到	dào	47
冂	4	内	nèi	48
	5	用	yòng	49
	6	同	tóng	50
	6	网	wǎng	51
八（丷）	2	八	bā	52
	4	分	fēn	53
	4	公	gōng	54
	5	半	bàn	55
	6	共	gòng	56
	6	关	guān	57
	7	弟	dì	58
	8	单	dān	59
	9	前	qián	60
	9	首	shǒu	61
	10	真	zhēn	62

人	2	人	rén	63
	4	今	jīn	64
	6	会	huì	65
	6	伞	sǎn	66
亻	4	化	huà	67
	5	们	men	68
	7	但	dàn	69
	7	你	nǐ	70
	7	体	tǐ	71
	7	位	wèi	72
	7	住	zhù	73
	8	使	shǐ	74
	10	候	hòu	75
	11	做	zuò	76
勹	5	包	bāo	77
儿	2	儿	ér	78
	4	元	yuán	79
	6	先	xiān	80
厶	4	云	yún	81
	5	去	qù	82
又	2	又	yòu	83
	4	双	shuāng	84
	4	友	yǒu	85
	5	对	duì	86
	5	发	fā/fà	87
	10	难	nán/nàn	88
力	2	力	lì	89
	4	办	bàn	90
	6	动	dòng	91
	7	努	nǔ	92
Three strokes				
氵	5	汉	hàn	93
	5	汁	zhī	94
	7	没	méi	95
	7	汽	qì	96
	8	法	fǎ	97
	8	河	hé	98

	9	活	huó	99
	10	酒	jiǔ	100
	16	澡	zǎo	101
忄	6	忙	máng	102
宀	6	安	ān	103
	7	完	wán	104
	8	定	dìng	105
	8	实	shí	106
	9	客	kè	107
	10	家	jiā	108
广	7	应	yìng/yīng	109
门	3	门	mén	110
	6	问	wèn	111
	7	间	jiān/jiàn	112
辶	5	边	biān	113
	6	达	dá	114
	7	还	huán/hái	115
	7	近	jìn	116
	7	运	yùn	117
	9	退	tuì	118
	12	道	dào	119
土	3	土	tǔ	120
艹	9	草	cǎo	121
	11	菜	cài	122
大	3	大	dà	123
	4	太	tài	124
	8	奇	qí	125
扌	5	打	dǎ	126
	6	扫	sǎo	127
	7	把	bà	128
	7	报	bào	129
小	3	小	xiǎo	130
	4	少	shǎo/shào	131
口	5	号	hào	132
	5	叫	jiào	133
	5	可	kě	134
	5	史	shǐ	135
	6	吃	chī	136

	6	后	hòu	137
	6	名	míng	138
	7	告	gào	139
	7	听	tīng	140
	8	和	hé	141
	11	唱	chàng	142
	12	喝	hē	143
口	5	四	sì	144
	6	回	huí	145
	6	团	tuán	146
	6	因	yīn	147
	8	国	guó	148
山	3	山	shān	149
彳	9	很	hěn	150
	11	得	dé	151
	12	街	jiē	152
彡	7	形	xíng	153
夕	5	外	wài	154
	6	多	duō	155
	14	舞	wǔ	156
夊	10	夏	xià	157
饣	7	饭	fàn	158
	8	饱	bǎo	159
	10	饿	è	160
己	3	己	jǐ	161
弓	7	张	zhāng	162
女	3	女	nǚ	163
	5	奶	nǎi	164
	6	好	hǎo/hào	165
	6	如	rú	166
	8	妻	qī	167
	8	姓	xìng	168
子	3	子	zǐ	169
	6	字	zì	170
	8	学	xué	171
	9	孩	hái	172
纟	8	练	liàn	173

	9	给	gěi	174
马	11	骑	qí	175
Four strokes				
灬	9	点	diǎn	176
	10	热	rè	177
	12	然	rán	178
文	4	文	wén	179
火	4	火	huǒ	180
	6	灯	dēng	181
心	4	心	xīn	182
	5	必	bì	183
	9	思	sī	184
	11	您	nín	185
	13	想	xiǎng	186
户	8	房	fáng	187
礻	8	视	shì	188
王	4	王	wáng	189
	11	理	lǐ	190
	11	球	qiú	191
木	4	木	mù	192
	5	本	běn	193
	7	李	lǐ	194
	7	条	tiáo	195
	8	果	guǒ	196
	10	根	gēn	197
	10	校	xiào	198
	12	椅	yǐ	199
犬	10	哭	kū	200
戈	7	我	wǒ	201
比	4	比	bǐ	202
止	5	正	zhèng	203
	7	步	bù	204
日	4	日	rì	205
	6	早	zǎo	206
	7	时	shí	207
	8	明	míng	208
	8	易	yì	209

	9	春	chūn	210
	9	是	shì	211
	9	星	xīng	212
	11	晚	wǎn	213
	12	普	pǔ	214
	12	最	zuì	215
	15	影	yǐng	216
贝	9	贵	guì	217
见	4	见	jiàn	218
	8	现	xiàn	219
	9	觉	jiào/jué	220
牛	4	牛	niú	221
手	4	手	shǒu	222
	10	拿	ná	223
气	4	气	qì	224
夂	11	敢	gǎn	225
	11	教	jiāo	226
	13	数	shǔ/shù	227
斤	13	新	xīn	228
爫	10	爱	ài	229
月	4	月	yuè	230
	6	有	yǒu	231
	8	服	fú	232
	8	朋	péng	233
	8	育	yù	234
	9	胖	pàng	235
	10	能	néng	236
	11	脚	jiǎo	237
风	4	风	fēng	238
水	4	水	shuǐ	239
	7	求	qiú	240
Five strokes				
母	7	每	měi	241
立	5	立	lì	242
	9	亲	qīn	243
	10	站	zhàn	244
衤	10	被	bèi	245

目	9	看	kàn/kān	246
	9	相	xiàng/xiāng	247
	11	眼	yǎn	248
田	5	电	diàn	249
	5	田	tián	250
	7	男	nán	251
	11	累	lèi	252
钅	10	钱	qián	253
	11	银	yín	254
矢	8	知	zhī	255
	12	短	duǎn	256
禾	9	秋	qiū	257
	9	香	xiāng	258
	9	种	zhòng/zhǒng	259
瓜	5	瓜	guā	260
鸟	5	鸟	niǎo	261
穴	8	空	kōng/kòng	262
	9	突	tū	263
	10	容	róng	264
Six strokes				
衣	6	衣	yī	265
	8	表	biǎo	266
羊	6	羊	yáng	267
	9	美	měi	268
米	6	米	mǐ	269
老	6	考	kǎo	270
	6	老	lǎo	271
耳	6	耳	ěr	272
页	6	页	yè	273
	9	须	xū	274
	15	题	tí	275
舌	11	甜	tián	276
	12	舒	shū	277
⺮	14	算	suàn	278
自	6	自	zì	279
舟	11	船	chuán	280
糸	7	系	xì	281

311

Seven strokes				
走	7	走	zǒu	282
	10	起	qǐ	283
	12	超	chāo	284
里	7	里	lǐ	285
足	7	足	zú	286
	12	跑	pǎo	287
	13	跟	gēn	288
	13	路	lù	289
	15	踢	tī	290
身	7	身	shēn	291
角	7	角	jiǎo	292
	13	解	jiě	293
豕	13	像	xiàng	294
Eight strokes				
金	8	金	jīn	295
雨	8	雨	yǔ	296
鱼	8	鱼	yú	297
	14	鲜	xiān/xiǎn	298
Nine strokes				
革	15	鞋	xié	299
食	9	食	shí	300

English and Chinese Characters Cross-references

English	Chinese Character	Page
ability; skill; energy able; capable can; be able to	能	236
accommodate; hold; contain; tolerate; permit; allow facial expression; appearance; looks	容	264
accuse; tell; appeal to	诉	36
again; then; once more; only then; in addition; on the top of that; no matter; how...still	再	13
ahead; earlier; at first; for the time being; before ancestor deceased	先	80
air; gas; breath; smell; weather; airs; manner; spirit; insult get angry; annoy	气	224
alcoholic drink; wine; liquor; spirits	酒	100
appear; show in time of need present, existing	现	219
appearance; outside; surface show; express	表	266
arrive; reach; go to up to; up until thoughtful	到	47
ask; inquire; exam	问	111
autumn; fall; harvest time; year; a period time	秋	257
ball; globe; anything shaped like a ball; ball game; the globe	球	191
bath; shower	澡	101
be able to; approve; may; good to; can; fit but	可	134
be full; plump; fully; satisfy	饱	159
beard; moustache must; have to	须	274

beg; demand; ask; pray; strike for; seek	求	240
behind; after; last; offspring; empress; queen	后	137
between; among; room; space	间	112
big; heavy; loud; major; eldest greatly; in a big way	大	123
bird	鸟	261
boat; ship	船	280
body; oneself; life	身	291
body; style; system; personally to do... ; put oneself in...	体	71
born; produce; give birth; be born; grow life; pupil; scholar alive; green; raw...	生	22
bright; clear; open; honest tomorrow; sight understand	明	208
broom; sweep; sweep away; eliminate; clean up	扫	127
bull; ox; cattle stubborn	牛	221
bun; bag; package wrap	包	77
business; matter; trouble; job; responsibility be engaged in; serve	事	15
busy; fully occupied hurry; hasten	忙	102
but; still; nevertheless only; merely	但	69
buy; purchase	买	28
capital of a country; short if Beijing	京	29
carry; transport; use motion; movement	运	117
centre; middle; in; among; intermediate; mean; half- way; in the process of... fit for hit	中	17
century; lifetime; life; generation; age; the world	世	12
chair	椅	199
change; exchange easy; amiable	易	209

change; turn; convert; melt; digest; burn up chemistry	化	67
character; script; writing; language; literature; culture civil; gentle; cover	文	179
character; word; form; writings; receipt; a style	字	170
child	儿	78
child	孩	172
clothes	衣	265
cloud say(only for Chinese classics)	云	81
comfort; stretch; unfold; spread leisurely	舒	277
common; general share together	共	56
compete; ratio; than contrast	比	202
complete; run out; end; finish; intact	完	104
count; be reckoned; numerate; list number; figure several; a few	数	227
count; calculate; reckon; include; plan; guess; consider at long last; in the end	算	278
country; state; nation	国	148
cry; weep; burst into tears	哭	200
currency; copper coin; money; cash; fund	钱	253
dance dance with sth; flourish	舞	156
dare courage brave	敢	225
dear; close parents; marriage; relatives; bride in person kiss	亲	243
delicious; beautiful; good; very satisfactory beautify; be pleased with oneself	美	268

English	Character	Number
difficult; hard; put something into a difficult position hardship disaster	难	88
diplomat; envoy; messenger use; make; send; cause	使	74
disappear; not have; there is not; be not so as; less than have not; did not	没	95
discuss; exchange views on; talk over opinion; view	议	34
dissect; separate; untie; dispel; explain; comprehend solution	解	293
divide minute; branch	分	53
do; make; produce; manufacture; cook; engage in; become; compose; be used as; for...	做	76
door; gate	门	110
drink	喝	143
drop; spot; dot stroke; point... drip; check one by one; light... a bit; time of o'clock	点	176
ear	耳	272
eat	吃	136
edge; side; bound; border while	边	113
eight	八	52
electricity; telegram; cable get an electronic shock	电	249
element; unit; component first; primary; basic; fundamental; principal	元	79
empty; hollow sky; air for nothing; in vain leave empty	空	262
evening; night late; younger	晚	213
every; each; per; each time; on each occasion; often	每	241
expensive; highly valued; of high rank	贵	217

experience; go through all previous covering all calendar	历	45
eye; a small hole; key point look	眼	248
face to; oppose; correct; deal with; brief; couple; with regard to	对	86
face; surface; side; noodle directly soft	面	16
farmland; field; cropland	田	250
fat; fatty	胖	235
few; little; less be short; lose; stop a little while; young early youth	少	131
fire; firearms; temper lose one's temper fiery; urgent	火	180
fish	鱼	297
flat; level; even; smooth make level; be on the same level; make the same score; equal; calm; put down; average	平	11
fly; flit; flutter	飞	26
food eat	食	300
foot enough; sufficient fully; as much as	足	286
foot; base	脚	237
four	四	144
fragrant; sweet-smelling; delicious; savoury; sound perfume; joss stick	香	258
fresh; bright-coloured; delicious; tasty delicacy; seafood rare	鲜	298
friend friendly	友	85
friend join together; gang up	朋	233

front; forward; ago; before; first proceeding; former; future	前	60
fruit; really if indeed	果	196
give to for	给	174
go; send there; remove; go in order to; in order to; be apart; away just gone of	去	82
gold; metal; money golden; precious	金	295
good; fine; be in good health; be good to; the better to; how like; love; be liable to	好	165
grass careless draft	草	121
group; regiment; ball roll something into a ball; unite round; circular	团	146
guest; visitor; traveller; customer; live in a strange place objective	客	107
half very little partly	半	55
Han nationality; the Han Dynasty; Chinese language	汉	93
hand handy personally	手	222
handle; a handful of; hold	把	128
harmony; peace kind draw together with; and	和	141
have; there is; exist	有	231
head; leader; chief first	首	61

head; top; end; beginning; chief; first; leading before	头	2
heart; mind; feelings; intention; centre; core	心	182
heat; fever; temperature; hot; warm hearted; popular; heat up	热	177
heel follow towards; and	跟	288
history	史	135
hold; seize; put; have a firm grasp by meaning of; as regard as	拿	223
home; family a specialist my domestic	家	108
home; lining; inside; inner; neighbourhood; native place mile in; inside	里	285
horn; bugle; corner; angle *jiao,* fractional unit of money in China	角	292
house; room	房	187
howl; bugle; horn number; date; name; mark	号	132
hungry hunger starve	饿	160
I; me; one; self; my	我	201
ice feel cold put ice around	冰	32
image; be like; look as if; such as; likeness; portrait; image; picture	像	294
inside; with; inner part; in; internal; one's wife	内	48
is over; finish; end; accomplished; at the last; know clearly; cannot stand for sth; entirely; completely	了	24
juice	汁	94
justice; human relationship; meaning righteous; adopted	义	1
kick; play	踢	290

king; monarch; duke	王	189
knowledge know; realize; inform	知	255
knowledge know	识	35
lamb; lantern; light	灯	181
language; words; tongue speak; say	语	39
launch; send out; utter; rise; open up; have a feeling; develop; discover; start... hairs measure word for bullets and shells	发	87
law; method; way; standard; model; magic arts follow; model after	法	97
leave; depart; keep away; be away from; without; inde- pendent of	离	31
listen; hear; heed; allow	听	140
little; small; young of short duration children	小	130
live; save alive; vivid; moving simply works	活	99
long; length; be good at... older; head; grow; being to grow; increase...	长	21
love; affection; be fond of	爱	229
main; primary host; owner; master; person; God manage; indicate; advocate	主	3
man; male; son; boy baron	男	251
manage; do; set up	办	90
manage; put in order; pay attention to reason; logic; natural science	理	190
many; have more; over a specified amount; how	多	155
medicine; treatment; cure; doctor	医	46
meet; get together; know; can; be able to; be good at; be likely to meeting; society; capital; a moment	会	65

320

melon	瓜	260
milk; breasts suckle; feed; breast	奶	164
miss; think; recall; suppose; want to; remember	想	186
moon; month full-month-shaped	月	230
morning early long ago	早	206
most	最	215
mountain; hill	山	149
move; act; change; use; touch	动	91
must; certainly; have to	必	183
name; fame; excuse given name; express famous	名	138
net; network; Internet catch with net	网	51
new; fresh; up-to date; brand new newly; recently	新	228
nine many; numerous	九	19
not; no	不	8
obey; serve; drink(medicine) clothes	服	232
obtain; get; gain; result in need; have to	得	151
old; experienced; tough old people overgrown for a long time; very; always	老	271
oneself; personal; one's own	己	161
open; lift; start; leave; write out; boil; make parts; potion	开	9
origin; stem; basis; native; according to	本	193
outer; outside other; foreign; unofficial besides	外	154
page	页	273
pair; dual; two; twin; both; even; double	双	84

peace; safety; calm set at ease; install	安	103
people; person; human; other; being an adult; every- one	人	63
people; the masses person of folk	民	27
picture; looks; appearance; posture; photograph see for oneself; look at; assist each other	相	247
place; position; location digit	位	72
plant; grow; cultivate seed; species; race kind; sort	种	259
please; invite; request; ask	请	41
plum; a Chinese surname	李	194
practice; train; drill; boil and scour raw silk; white silk; experienced; skilled	练	173
practice; be used to habit; custom	习	25
public; general; common; equitable official make public	公	54
put forth; bulge	努	92
quilt; cover a passive code	被	245
rain	雨	296
raise; educate; cultivate; give birth; nourish	育	234
raise; lift; elect; start; cite act; deed; move entire	举	4
reach; express eminent; distinguished	达	114
read; read aloud; attend school; study	读	40
reason; cause follow; carry on because of because	因	147

English	Character	Page
remember; write down notes; mark; sign	记	33
repetition; once more; also; and; again; in addition; both ...and...	又	83
report; repay newspaper	报	129
reside; live; stay; stop; firmly	住	73
respond; answer; comply with; suit; cope with	应	109
retreat; draw back cancel	退	118
return; go back still; even more; also; passably give or do sth.	还	115
return; turn to; answer to; report back; decline chapter; time	回	145
rice; food; meal	饭	158
rice; metre	米	269
ride horse; horse rider	骑	175
right; correct so; like that but; nevertheless; however	然	178
right; upright; honest; standard; regular; positive; correct... straiten; correct... just; right...	正	203
rise; get up; remove; appear; grow; build; set up; start; up	起	283
river	河	98
root completely	根	197
run; run a race; run about doing something; away	跑	287
school; field officer editing; correcting	校	198
see; look at; regard; look upon; inspect	视	188
see; read; consider; look; watch; call on; depend on; mind look after; keep an eye on	看	246
see; watch; meet with; appear to be; refer to view; opinion	见	218

self; oneself; one's own certainly; of course from; since	自	279
sell; betray; exert to the utmost; show off	卖	43
seven	七	5
shadow; reflection; trace; photograph; film	影	216
shape; form; body appear; contrast	形	153
sheep; goat	羊	267
shoes	鞋	299
short; brief lack weak point	短	256
shortcut; nearby; access; close; approaching; intimate	近	116
shut; close mountain pass	关	57
silver; relating to currency; silver-coloured	银	254
similar; be like; as; as if; be as sth as; such as; for instance if; in case(of); in the event of	如	166
sing	唱	142
single; one; thin; simple only; alone sheet; bill	单	59
sky; heavens; day; a period of time in the day; season; weather; nature; God natural; inborn	天	10
sleep sense; feel; wake up; awake; become aware	觉	220
soil; earth; land local; homemade; unrefined	土	120
solid; practical; true; real reality; fruit	实	106
son; child; person; seed you young	子	169
south	南	44
speak; talk; say; explain; scold theory	说	38
spread; open; stretch; set out; magnify; look a popular surname	张	162

324

spring; love; life	春	210
stable; fixed; calm decide; subscribe certainly; definitely	定	105
stand; be on one's feet; stop station; stop; service	站	244
stand; erect; set; establish; conclude upright immediately	立	242
star; bit	星	212
steam; vapour	汽	96
step; pace walk	步	204
strange; rare; remarkable be surprised very; extremely odd number	奇	125
street; road; market	街	152
strength; force; power do all one can; make every effort	力	89
strike; hit; break; smash; heat... from; since	打	126
study; imitate learning; knowledge	学	171
subject; topic; title inscribe	题	275
suddenly; abruptly; unexpectedly dash forward; charge into; sticking out	突	263
summer	夏	157
sun; daytime; day; time daily	日	205
surname be called	姓	168
surpass; exceed; take a short cut	超	284
sweet; sound	甜	276
tall; high; loud	高	30
teach; instruct; educate religion	教	226
tell; accuse ; ask for; declare	告	139
test; exam; check; inspect; study; investigate	考	270

thank; make an apology decline; wither	谢	42
think; consider; think of thought; thinking	思	184
thousand; a great amount of	千	20
tie; bind; fasten; to be system; department	系	281
time; times; season; opportunity current now and then; from time to time	时	207
tired; weary; fatigued tire; wear out; work hard	累	252
to be; correct; right be just right	是	211
today; modern; now; present	今	64
together same; alike; similar; be the same as with; and	同	50
too; greatest	太	124
true; real; clear really; truly; indeed	真	62
trunk; dry do dried objects	干	6
twig; note; strip; item; order	条	195
two; a few; some both; either; neither a traditional unit of weight 50 grams	两	14
umbrella	伞	66
universal; general	普	214
up; upper; higher; last; most; recent; first come up; get on; go to; go ahead; enter; supply; be carried on; be engaged... on; within; in; at; formerly; above; up...	上	7
use; need; eat; drink expenses; usefulness with	用	49
vegetable; food; dish	菜	122
very; very much; quite	很	150
wait; await time; season	候	75

walk; go; run; move; leave; visit; through; escape; depart from...	走	282
water; river; waters; a liquid	水	239
way; road; doctrine a measure word	道	119
way; road; path; journey; line; region; route; sort; grade	路	289
we; you; they; ours; yours... (plural suffix for mankind)	们	68
wife	妻	167
wind; practice; custom; style rumoured; unfounded	风	238
woman; female; daughter; girl	女	163
wood; tree; timber made of wood; simple; wooden; numb	木	192
word; talk talk about; speak about	话	37
wrong; not conform to; non-; have got to	非	18
year; age; a period in one's life; a period in history; harvest; New Year annual; yearly	年	23
yell; shout; cry; call; order; ask; name; allow	叫	133
you	你	70
you(polite form)	您	185
younger brother	弟	58